The Six-Step Revision Process

Revise Your Novel from First Draft to Final

Miranda Darrow

Publisher's Cataloging-in-Publication data

Names: Darrow, Miranda, author.

Title: The six-step revision process: revise your novel from first draft to final / Miranda Darrow.

Series: Concise Fiction Academy

Description: Little Falls, MN: Miranda Darrow, LLC, 2024.

Identifiers: LCCN: 2024913436 | ISBN: 979-8-9909804-3-3 (paperback) | 979-8-9909804-2-6 (ebook) | 979-8-9909804-4-0 (audio)
Subjects: LCSH Fiction--Authorship. | Fiction--Technique. | Creative writing. | BISAC LANGUAGE ARTS & DISCIPLINES / Editing & Proofreading | LANGUAGE ARTS & DISCIPLINES / Grammar & Punctuation | LANGUAGE ARTS & DISCIPLINES / Writing / Fiction Writing | LANGUAGE ARTS & DISCIPLINES / Writing / Authorship
Classification: LCC PN3355 .D37 2024 | DDC 808.3--dc23

Contents

Introduction

How to use this resource

Welcome, writer, to a light-hearted look at a serious topic: how to get your manuscript in its best possible shape on your own, or with minimal professional assistance. This book is for writers who want to tackle self-editing, whether for one book or one each month. I see you, high-output indie authors, out there writing books and running a business.

The goal is efficiency so you aren't wasting time editing a section that ends up on the cutting room floor. We'll take a top-down approach, tackling the biggest picture issues first and then digging into more granular details so you don't spend valuable time re-arranging the deck chairs on the Titanic.

This writing craft guide will touch on topics worthy of their own books: pacing, dialogue, "show, don't tell" (SDT), etc. To keep this title in an easily digestible manual that you can breeze through to quickly locate the next steps, we'll delve into each of these issues in turn and point you to additional resources. The point of this craft book isn't to give in-depth explanations of each of the overlapping topics. Instead, the goal is to organize these concepts for you so you can approach revisions methodically.

This book is a framework that will point you in the right direction when you need more resources to up specific parts of your game.

It's a roadmap for your revisions.

Roadmap
to
Revisions

Map your progress in each step.

For each of the six steps, I'll start with an updated image of the Roadmap to Revisions with a flag showing where you are in the process. There are many methods for revising your novel. I start at the chapter or scene level and work on macro-level issues first, then move to the paragraph level, and end with line-level edits of your polished manuscript, ready for querying or self-publishing. I've compiled this information based on presentations I've given at multiple writing conferences and integrated lessons I've learned while presenting on this topic to writing groups.

Different writers enjoy various aspects of the process more than others. Discovery writers often love the thrill of experiencing their story as they write their first draft. Plotters may savor brainstorming, tossing around ideas, or working on an outline or even (gasp!) a synopsis before they sit down to write. Social butterflies may enjoy the critique partner swap phase, giving feedback on their critique partner's current work in progress (WIP) while the critique partner is roughing up their precious baby with gentle suggestions (and, hopefully, some kudos). And then there are the authors who *love* revising. (Confession: I am not one of those writers.) At a recent conference, I polled conference attendees to tell me their favorite part of the writing process. I was surprised when 44% picked revising.

Regardless of whether you enjoy revising, this book can help you be more efficient at it. This resource can assist pantsers (who write by the "seat of their pants") or plotters (who outline the plot before writing) and writers who fall somewhere in between (plantsers). Feel free to adapt this process to work for you.

For most writers, revising your manuscript is a necessity. Why do I say "most" instead of all?

I've got two campsites available at Camp No Revisions:

1. I'm writing for a narrow audience of readers

who aren't expecting a polished manuscript.

2. I'm a freaking writing genius.

*One of my decorative
campers.*

First, we have the limited-audience campsite.
These writers can truthfully say, "I'm writing for
myself and/or my family and close personal friends.
I'm not getting an agent or listing this for sale
online. This book (often memoir or family history)
is my therapy, my hobby, something I want to leave
for my kids/grandkids/future generations." To those
authors, I say, "Carry on! If you ever change your
mind and seek a wider audience for your work,
join the rest of us in revision purgatory—oh, wait, I
mean the enjoyable process of bringing out the best
version of your manuscript."

Second, we have the campsite for the Doogie
Howsers of writing (or Doogie Kamealohas, for the

younger crowd). There may be some author savant who writes publishable prose with every tap of the keyboard, a Mozart of manuscripts. Hey, in a multi-verse, everything is possible.

If you're reading this book, you already know that revision is necessary to get to the best version of your manuscript. Frequently, first drafts are how authors tell the story to themselves. My first drafts look more like screenplays than novels, with lots of dialogue and awkward setting cues. I've read other first drafts with nothing but worldbuilding—who needs plot? (Spoiler: readers do.) Readers need a well-developed plot and a well-rounded story, so revise we must. There's a rumor that many agents are closed to queries in December to avoid submissions from writers who won NaNoWriMo in November. Yes, you can write 50,000 words in a month. But that is a first draft, not a novel that is ready to query. So, on to the revision process.

Here are the Six Steps:

1. The Big Chart

2. Work the Chart

3. Add Depth

4. Get Feedback and Incorporate

5. Line Revisions

6. What's Next

The goal of this exercise is to generate a personalized checklist so you can see progress as you revise. Your process will involve interim goals and milestones so you can have a celebration each time you complete a step. Well, as much of a party as I throw, since I'm a morning bird who likes to be in bed by 9 p.m. Party on!

Speaking of celebrations, when you finish your first draft of a manuscript, you've done more than almost everyone who wants to write a book. All those people at that coworker's dinner party, the neighborhood bunco league, or the family cookout, yammering on about how they're going to write their magnum opus one of these days. It's going to blow your book out of the water. Most of them will *never* write a complete novel. One statistic I found online said that **97%** of people who start writing a novel never finish. And you know it must be true because it was on the internet. [/sarcasm]

But *you've* done it. You've written a novel. There's a beginning, a middle, and even an end. That makes you a novelist. Yes, there may be some plot holes in this road but that's what we're going to work on together. **Take a moment to celebrate this accomplishment!**

Even though there are six steps, my method only has four drafts. Some steps don't require revisions. Hooray! And if you haven't yet finished your first draft, that's okay. You can jump in with a partial manuscript to work on the first steps (especially Step One, making the Big Chart), as that can help get you "unstuck" and back on track. You'll need to spend more time in those early steps, as you want a fully developed story before moving past Step Two.

How much time will this take?

How long an author needs to spend on each step depends on the scope of structural changes needed (which can be related to whether there was an intentional effort at plotting either before or during the drafting process). My theory on pantsers versus plotters is that at some point, every author needs to spend some time with their plot. You can either do it upfront and work from an already-plotted outline, or you can "discovery write" ("pants") your way through and do more work on the back end hammering structure into your already-drafted WIP.

When I was presenting on this topic at the Women's Fiction Writers Association (WFWA) conference, I was in the hotel's main ballroom, presenting to my biggest writing group audience to date. I looked at the audience and saw a bestselling women's fiction author whom I adore. (Okay, I have no chill. It was Kristan Higgins, y'all.) I had about two seconds of imposter syndrome brain freeze and then I remembered I'm Miranda Freaking Darrow (not my actual middle name). I am not a shrinking violet.

At the end of my presentation, Ms. Higgins asked me, "How long does this revision process take?"

I answered, "Assuming your critique partners get back to you within two weeks, I'd say about six weeks."

Boom, an answer. Only she knows if this was accurate. But my point is your turnaround time for getting feedback from your critique partners and/or beta readers in Step Four is a main contributing factor to how quickly you can complete all six steps.

The Six-Step Revision Process is malleable. It can go as fast or as slow as you push it along. If you're a plotter (especially if you already have a chapter outline), Step One may be mostly done already. If you have critique partners on lock, you could be done fast. But, if your plot is as holey as Swiss cheese and you need to figure things out for the book to come together, then take that time. Your story and your readers will thank you for it. Alter these steps to suit your needs as an author.

Whether this is your first novel or your hundredth, spending the time you need to hammer out the plot, the character arcs, the worldbuilding, and more—and then reading through it again to work on active voice, SDT, continuity—*all of this* (picture me waving my hands so vigorously that my smart watch counts it as exercise) will improve your novel and solidify your relationship with your readers. Impressing your readers with the power and professionalism in your story is the best way to grow your reader base. Well, that and viral TikTok videos, but I can't help you there. I'm running an online-based freelance editing business despite my social media skills, not because of them. Nonetheless, having a well-revised and carefully edited book is worth the effort.

We're ready to start Step One! As bonus content, I've included a decision tree: if you can pass all five inquiries, you're ready to revise. If there are a few that you acknowledge could use some work, keep those in mind when working through Step One. You will want to identify your main character and their character flaw as part of Step One and Step Two. And question five, about your readiness—that's a free square on your bingo card. You are reading this book for a reason—you're ready to bring out the best version of your WIP.

Bonus Content: A Revision Readiness Decision Tree

Are you ready for the Six-Step Revision Process?

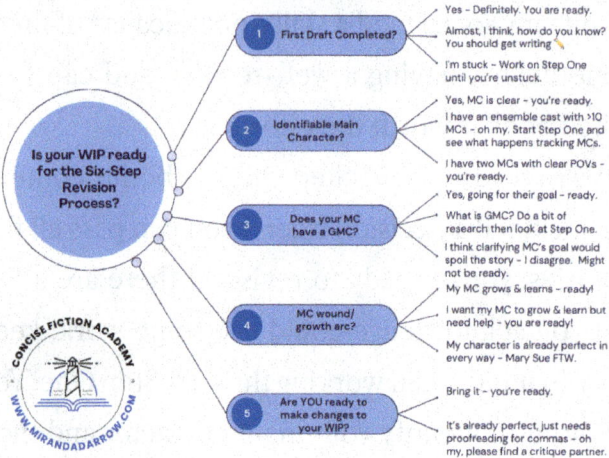

Is your WIP ready for the Six-Step Revision Process?

1. First Draft Completed?
- Yes – Definitely. You are ready.
- Almost, I think, how do you know? You should get writing ✏
- I'm stuck – Work on Step One until you're unstuck.

2. Identifiable Main Character?
- Yes, MC is clear – you're ready.
- I have an ensemble cast with >10 MCs - oh my. Start Step One and see what happens tracking MCs.
- I have two MCs with clear POVs - you're ready.

3. Does your MC have a GMC?
- Yes, going for their goal – ready.
- What is GMC? Do a bit of research then look at Step One.
- I think clarifying MC's goal would spoil the story – I disagree. Might not be ready.

4. MC wound/ growth arc?
- My MC grows & learns – ready!
- I want my MC to grow & learn but need help – you are ready!
- My character is already perfect in every way – Mary Sue FTW.

5. Are YOU ready to make changes to your WIP?
- Bring it – you're ready.
- It's already perfect, just needs proofreading for commas – oh my, please find a critique partner.

CONCISE FICTION ACADEMY

WWW.MIRANDADARROW.COM

Step One

The Big Chart

Where are we on the revision roadmap? We're near the beginning, but Step One doesn't start at square one. It's four spaces in, as you've already come up with the amazing story idea, written the manuscript (*wow*, you did that!), and decided to revise your WIP. Those are three big steps toward having a polished novel ready for the world. Sometimes these preliminary steps before Step One can feel insurmountable, like you'll never be ready to revise your WIP. Spinning in a circle and tying yourself into a mental knot aren't "required" steps. But I've yet to meet a writer who doesn't have a tale about the time they made no progress for months, if not years, on a tricky WIP.

Step 1-
Make the
Big Chart

Notice we're starting several spaces in, as you've already written your first draft.

Step One is making a "Big Chart" showing all the scenes in your WIP and mapping out what's happening. The goal in Step One is to document your current draft on a scene/chapter level, capture the plot points, character development arcs, and major subplots of your novel. This is a big task and can be tedious. I recommend finishing your chart *before* you start revising (Step Two). Story issues you identify later in the manuscript could change your plan depending on later chapters/scenes. The goal of this Six-Step Revision Process is to avoid unnecessary revisions and *not* waste time on parts that end up on the cutting room floor.

Let's start with the electronic/computer-based Big Chart options. I'd say the Big Chart is the best way to view your novel "at a glance" but unless you have fly eyes or a panoramic lens, it's tough to see your whole chart in one glance. My longest chart was 56 pages on legal-sized paper. I could have wallpapered my office with it. It was a beast but it helped me strike the right balance between multiple subplots and two character growth arcs, oh my! For my clients, I often create a table in Microsoft Word, since that way I can see all the content and it's easy to email.

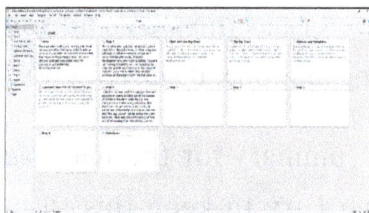

Screenshot of a Scrivener corkboard

Let's talk about columns and rows for this Big Chart. For the columns: I start with a few column headings (usually five to six). Sometimes it's tricky to pick the "right" columns and we end up adding one (or abandoning one) partway through—that's okay. The rows are easier because that's one for each chapter (or scene, if you have multiple scenes in your chapters).

These columns could be:

1. Chapter number and story timeline: the timeline could be calendar days or days starting from chapter 1, such as five days later with a running total, and then whatever hints or clues we have about the season and time of year.

2. POV: if the manuscript has multiple POV characters, the next column tracks which character has the POV and sometimes the setting (optional if single POV).

3. Plot summary for the main action in the scene: I try to keep this to two to three sentences with just the main plot, excluding the subplots. I also teach a class on writing a synopsis—one tip is starting with this row in

a Big Chart and taking out things that aren't vitally important.

4. Subplot #1: this could be a romance subplot (tracking the romance beats), or a mystery (keeping track of when clues and red herrings are dropped and who knows them). There could be two (or more) columns to track subplots.

5. Character growth arc: in a romance, this could be captured for both leads in a "romance subplot" column. For other stories, especially women's fiction or YA with a central character growth arc, it deserves a column of its own.

6. Changes to be made in the next round of revisions: this is your call to action in Step Two. This column can be left blank while you're working through the scenes.

Here's a chart using Sally and Hector's story that I use for examples throughout the book:

chapter / timeline	POV character – growth arc	main story plot	romance plot	changes needed
Chapter 1 / scene 1 / first week in Sept	MC intro GMC – Sally wants to prove she's independent and doesn't need help	first big event - Weasels attack the town and eat the village's silo of grain	not yet introduced	
Chapter 1 / scene 2 / same day	Love Interest intro – Hector moves to town and opens an animal sanctuary	the townspeople think the weasels came from Hector's farm	Meet Cute – Hector meets Sally when she leads an angry mob to his farm with torches and pitchforks	

Screenshot of a sample big chart.

List your column headers in the first row (and if your platform has the option, "pin" this row to the top of all future pages so you can always see the column headings). After the header row, add a row for each chapter or scene. How many rows you need is directly related to how many chapters or scenes you have and need to track. But don't be deceived by how skinny those rows start. In Word and other formats that show all the content, this chart will expand and take over your screen, even if you switch to Landscape perspective (which I recommend) and if you use a paper size that is unprintable by anyone without a professional printer. I'd need a monitor the size of a Jumbotron to display some of my Big Charts. This chart can be in Word, Excel, Google Docs, Google Sheets, Scrivener, Plottr, Lucid Spark, and other programs. If you've found one that works for you which I haven't mentioned, drop me a line at miranda@mirandadarrow.com. I'm always looking for new resources.

And now, for the Luddites and people who kick it old school (myself included), low-tech Big Chart options. I've revised one of my manuscripts by using a fancy, dedicated notebook with tabs for each chapter. I wrote down the plot points, character growth arc milestones, and revolving POVs with fancy pens and tape flags. I was in office supply heaven! But it wasn't searchable. It was satisfying but the least adaptable of the Big Chart methods I've used. I'll just need to find other uses for the dozens of fancy notebooks I've collected that I've deemed "too nice" for everyday use.

Somewhat more flexible—and a method I still use today—is index cards and a corkboard or whiteboard (ideally a metal one that works with magnets). The output of this method is tough to send to a client. It's not very professional to send clients a series of pictures they'd need to piece together like a jigsaw puzzle to recreate the full chart. Case in point:

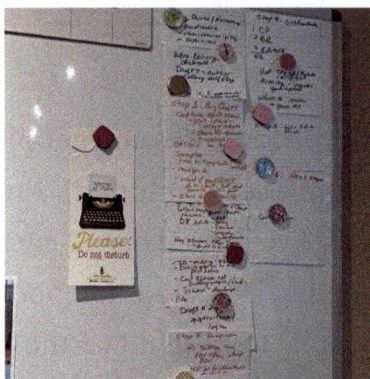

Actual whiteboard and index card chart for this book, early version.

Are you a fan of low-tech solutions? Get creative, and stick Post-Its on your door, create a DIY murder board—the sky's the limit. I recommend this approach for memoirs or stories told out of order because you can move the chapters/scenes/vignettes around and build a logical framework to pull them into a cohesive narrative by sliding cards around the whiteboard. Yes, you can do this with Scrivener too. That program's full capabilities are beyond my tech skills and I'm always afraid a scene card could "disappear" into the ether. That won't happen with note cards on a whiteboard. However, I have dropped them off the board and needed to move my low bookcase to retrieve them. It's the only time that area gets dusted, so it probably isn't a bad thing.

Work that final column – "Revisions Needed." Whether you're compiling your chart in an online document or spreadsheet, kicking it old school with scraps of paper and twine, or cracking open a dedicated notebook, the process will take time and effort.

Booker got tuckered out compiling his Big Chart.

The final part of Step One is to walk through the chart and note where there are plot jumps, gaps, holes, or three scenes in a row that all do the same thing. If you notice something while you're still working through the chapters, write it down then so you don't forget it. Brilliant insights should always be captured as quickly as possible, I say, as a person who routinely emails myself in the middle of the night from my phone so I don't forget my late-night flashes of brilliance.

What are we looking for here?

- Subplots that don't tie into the main plot or character growth arc.

- Multiple characters fulfilling the same role in the story who could be merged.

- A subplot—or worse, a main plot—that isn't resolved in the story.

- Loose ends and big continuity errors.

- Characters who are doing things that don't make sense (e.g. contradict their goal, motivation, and conflict—discussed more in Step Two).

Review your chart to track your plot points. Note when a key event happens "off the page" and readers are told about it after the fact. When you find one, add a row and brainstorm what you need in that new scene. While working through the scenes, also note any plot holes, inconsistencies, or major failings of that scene. Is it missing a setting? Did we lose track of a character or two? Make notes in your "Revisions Needed" column and tackle those in Step Two.

When you finish working through your Big Chart, in whatever format works best for you (or works best for this WIP), it's time to celebrate often the toughest step in the Six-Step Revision Process. Do *not* throw away this chart, even when you finish Step Two. Any time that you get feedback going forward (like in Step Four) and want to make big-picture revisions, this chart will be your best friend. It will let you know which plot points impact which scenes and can be your divining rod to guide your revisions, turning your efforts into a strategic strike rather than an endless game of hide-and-seek. And to get you on your way, the Bonus Content for Step One is a series of downloadable and customizable template Big Charts (Word, Google Docs, Excel, and Google Sheets), linked in Chapter 8.

Bonus Content: Template Big Charts

A10   ▼   ƒx   Notes about your revision plan, areas of concern to watch for, etc.:

	A	B	C	D	E
1					
2					**BOOK MD EDITING**
3					
4					
5					
6	To: AUTHOR				
7	From: Miranda Darrow, Book MD Editing				
8	Re: Chapter Chart for *WIP*				
9	Date: September 22. 2024				
10	Notes about your revision plan, areas of concern to watch for, etc.:				
11					
12	Chapter / timeline	POV Character – growth arc in chapter	Main Plot Chapter Events	Subplot main events	Recommendations
13	1. June 1.	Sally – wants to prove she is independent Misbelief, it would be weakness to accept help	Weasels attack the town and eat the village's silo of grain		
14					
15	2. Same day, later in the afternoon	Hector just moved to town and opened an animal sanctuary	The townspeople think the weasels came from Hector's sanctuary	Meet cute – Sally leads an angry mob to Hector's farm	
16					
17					
18					
19					
20					
21					
22					

Step Two

Work the Chart

In Step Two, we develop the list of revisions, your "to-do" list, and then we "do" them. Sorry, there aren't magical elves sneaking into our shoe shops at night to do these revisions for us. But we'll have a plan and some funky tools to help. First, let's check in with the Revision Roadmap. Here we are, starting Step Two where the focus is structural/big picture issues, taking in the entire forest before we investigate individual trees.

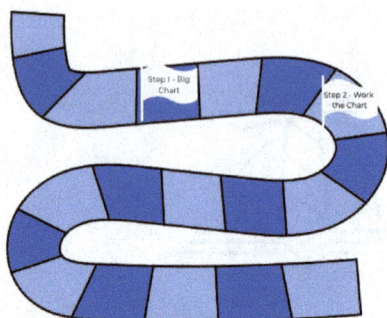

Step 2-
Work the
Chart

"Big Picture"
revisions/developmental
or substantive edits.

Let's start with that forest. From your Big Chart, list notes in the "Revisions Needed" column:

- Scenes you need to add

- Scenes to delete (and fixes you need to implement to preserve continuity)

Changes to enhance the plot:

- Remove subplots that aren't supporting the main plot

- Build out character growth arcs

- Add backstory to reinforce character and build in a basis for an emotional wound

- Watch for story beats and pacing

This is your starting point for your revisions to-do list for Step Two, but the list will evolve as you "get in there" revising, so don't laminate this list yet. I was living the dream when we got a label maker a few years back. It's a life goal to have a laminator for anything I want pressed in plastic so it won't get destroyed when I inevitably spill a beverage. Until then, this to-do list of revisions is a fluid document.

Let's talk about "Rehoming Your Darlings." This is a no-kill shelter for your previous words. No scenes or even lines need to be sacrificed. But they may need to be relocated out of your WIP. The best version of your novel may be buried under unnecessary subplots and "darling" scenes. It's time to be ruthless. Any scene that isn't advancing the main plot, a major subplot, or showing character growth is merely taking up space. Either integrate plot progress or character growth into that scene or cut the scene. Yes, it hurts, but nothing needs to disappear forever. We're relocating them outside of this manuscript, sending them to a very nice farm where they can run and play with other deleted scenes.

Pepper before and after her first haircut.

Here's my "Rehome Your Darlings" process:

- Save Version 1 of your full manuscript before making revisions. Make your revisions in a new document—Version 1 could become a collector's item someday!

- Start a new document with a festive name like Future Gold or Buried Treasure and copy/paste in parts you want to keep outside of your WIP.

- When you're looking for website content, newsletter articles, or bonus material, mine this extras document. It can also be the start of a novella or a freestanding short story in the same universe, a side plot for your characters.

- Or, swap out those character names and other details and save this scene for a different book/story universe.

Revise to address the big picture/plot issues. In this first revision, work through your chart and go scene-by-scene, building out all the changes you noted in the chart. Cut the scenes that don't serve your story and you won't waste more time and effort revising them.

Smooth out your story so it's coherent and decently polished.

1. Focus on what is happening in each scene: is it logical/reasonable/consistent for your characters to do it, here and in this way?

2. If readers are asking "why" then they may give up on your character as unlikeable or illogical.

3. Identify the "missing pieces" in your main plot, major subplot(s), and character growth arc, including key events that happen off the page.

4. Add a new line on your chart as a placeholder to add missing elements/brainstorm to fill gaps, then draft them.

5. Focus on key scenes and necessary transitions—cut "dear diary, today I waited, again, for that letter" or "I drove to Dubuque and thought about stuff" passages.

I use "driving to Dubuque" as my example of a scene where nothing of note is happening because I went to college in central Iowa and my parents lived in Wisconsin. There was a whole lot of corn and very little else to see on that drive along Highway 20. Dubuque is scenic, rolling hills, bluffs, and the Mississippi River, but getting there from the west—please use the Cliff Notes version.

By parents' house in Wisconsin, nearly Iowa.

Later, when we talk a bit more on the topic of "Show, Don't Tell," I give two examples of when it's preferable to tell readers in summary form in the narrative text. Traveling without incident is one of those times. Just be there. We're in Dubuque. Hooray!

I love suggesting clients *show* a pivotal scene on the page rather than *tell* readers about it after the fact. Authors usually go, "Of course! Why didn't I think of that?" My trick for identifying a missing key scene is any time a scene starts with a bunch of characters standing around talking about something that just happened—there it is. You missed it by that much. Show the scene where the thing happened, rather than telling us what happened through people talking about it. Seeing that scene live on the page is more impactful than hearing about it later.

Plot, pacing, and proportion: We'll tackle these three together since they are interrelated.

First, some definitions:

- **Plot** is "what is happening" to the characters in your story. It isn't the theme, moral, or the mood—it's literally x happened, then y, then z.

- **Pacing** is the speed at which the story is unfurling, whether clues are revealed every chapter or a slow build.

- **Proportion** is the amount of attention a character, plot point, or worldbuilding element is getting in the story.

These latter two concepts overlap and impact the story's plot and/or subplots. When something feels "off," but you (or your beta readers) can't figure out what it is, it often comes down to pacing and proportion and how they interact with plot.

Plot: I love books on plotting methods. My favorites are *Story Genius* by Lisa Cron, *Save the Cat Writes a Novel* by Jessica Brody, *How to Write a Novel Using the Snowflake Method* by Randy Ingermanson, and (for romance novels) *Romancing the Beat* by Gwen Hayes.

How do you evaluate your plot?

- Put yourself in the shoes of your future reader

- Try to forget everything you already know about the story

- Read down the column in your Big Chart that lists the main plot events and ask:

  - Are there gaps in logic or holes in the plot?

  - Are the events in your story logical and plausible, even in the context of a fictional universe?

  - Does this story make sense?

- Work through your main plot column and then each subplot

- Make sure your subplots have a logical progression **and** a tie into the main plot (eventually)

For example, Sally is the newly elected mayor, and the city is preparing for its Sweet Corn Days festival. Farmer Klein stops by the Mayor's office to complain about damage to his sweet corn crop—it looks like weasels from a newly relocated animal rescue operation have gotten onto his farm. Sally gathers a welcome wagon to check out the location. They show up and Hector, the owner of the animal rescue, greets them. Sally and Klein stomp around and find a hole in Hector's chicken wire fence big enough for rodents to escape. What does Hector do?

Does he:

- Offer to repair the fence? That sounds reasonable. Even if Klein isn't satisfied, Hector's response is related to the previous plot point and in alignment with his GMC.

- Threaten to run them over with his tractor? That seems rather drastic this early in the story, unless we know something in Hector's backstory to explain this escalation. We might be missing some necessary scenes before we get to this.

- Offer to teach them the electric slide? That would be tricky to justify logically unless this whole town is just waiting to get down, boogie woogie oogie.

Pacing: on a big-picture level, pacing is how fast the action and scenes are coming at readers. The Big Chart can help map where the **action** is happening, and then where characters catch their breath (and where readers can, too). It's important to allow for an interlude between action scenes—opportunities to show character growth arcs, theme, foreshadowing, etc. This is how action writers can have fully developed dynamic characters and not some "explosion here, explosion there" story that reads like a Transformers movie.

Slow pacing makes Pepper sleepy.

With literary-style fiction, the challenge is having enough scenes (and enough action) to keep driving the plot forward. Don't spend too much time (especially too many consecutive pages) stuck in the protagonist's head contemplating the universe or passively discussing things with other characters (a setup which would lack conflict and action). Even in a quiet story, a bit of micro-tension—for example, having conflicting goals for multiple characters in a scene—can go a long way to transform a scene from a soggy middle to an essential element of the story that propels the reader onward.

Proportion: This subjective and often not an issue. When proportion is a problem, it's usually a side character stealing every scene, or a subplot getting more attention than the purported main plot. If you have a problem with proportion—more words dedicated

Is Booker getting too much attention?

to a side character or plot—ask whether you're focusing your WIP on the right character, the right main plot, etc. Consider flipping the story on its head and telling it from that character's perspective. Or tone down the attention in this story and plan to write a sequel or another story in the same universe that features that charismatic side character or yummy subplot.

Measure how many words are dedicated to this side character or plot and see whether it corresponds with what you would expect from a story starring other characters or featuring another plot. Proportion can also come up with genre expectations. For example, if a writer spends more time describing their setting than readers expect in a contemporary story—or not enough time with worldbuilding if the book is pitched as hard sci-fi or high fantasy—then readers can be disappointed.

Let's take a peek at POV, perspective, and verb tense.

- Does your POV fit with your age category, genre, and the type of story you're writing?

- Is the POV consistent and (mostly) free of head-hopping?

- If there's more than one POV character:

  - Does every POV character have a unique narrative voice?

  - Are there logical transitions between characters?

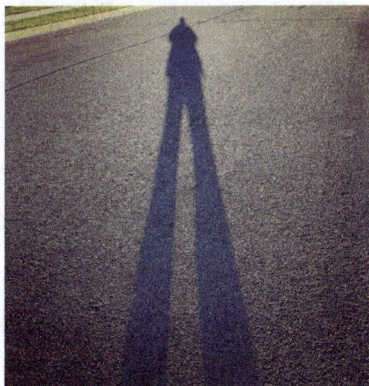

*My shadow, tall enough to
reach the high shelf.*

If you're considering a POV and/or verb tense change, do it in Step Two. This change will impact every chapter in the story. Go for it. Get it done now, so your Step Four readers can help you catch any misses—it's nearly impossible to change POV or verb tense without missing something at the line level (and often many somethings). Additionally, if you've written your manuscript in omniscient POV, here's your invitation to rethink that decision. My top craft book on POV is Alicia Rasley's *The Power of Point of View.*

Additional Big Picture revisions.

Big picture/developmental editing also evaluates:

- Character and growth arcs: do you have a multi-dimensional main character (not just a caricature or stereotype)? Does your main character have a misbelief they need to overcome? What are the steps they need to take to confront that notion and grow, becoming a changed person as a result?

- GMC (goal, motivation, and conflict): GMC is the engine that drives your story forward. Without GMC and sufficient conflict (even if it's micro-tension) in every scene, your manuscript might die from a fatal case of the doldrums. Let's toss stakes in here too.

- Setting: is the setting clear and consistent, both in location and time? This is especially important in science fiction, fantasy, and historical novels, but setting is important for all genres. Readers want the stories to exist somewhere, not just characters floating in the ether.

- Genre norms: I *highly* recommend reading new releases (within the last five years) in your genre and finding critique partners who write in your genre. So many authors comp to the classics, be it Jane Austen, Agatha Christie, or Kurt Vonnegut. I have read and enjoyed all three. But those are not current titles and not what today's readers expect.

Each of these topics headline craft books. I'll give an overview and my recommended books on these topics. Let me know if you want a Concise Fiction Academy treatment of a subject, since these books are substantial.

Characters and Growth Arcs: Do your characters seem like real people, and are they interesting enough for a reader to invest hours of their time following their adventure? A character does not have to be likeable—see *Gone Girl* and other books with unreliable narrators, like *Stone Cold Fox* by Rachel Koller Croft and *My Lovely Wife* by Samantha Downing. Unlikeable main characters play differently in different genres.

Make sure that your characters are not all the same person with the same (often the author's) personality. Your main characters should have dimension, depth, and quirks. Make sure they're not stereotypes. Main characters should have identifiable goals (discussed more in the section on GMC). Some writers inject differentiation between characters by assigning them personality types, like the Myers-Briggs Type Indicator (MBTI), Enneagram designations, DiSC personality types, or StrengthFinders.

As for growth arcs, most of my editing clients write character-driven fiction, such as book club/women's fiction, romance, young adult, contemporary, or literary fiction. Most of the mystery and speculative fiction I work with is also character-driven. Almost all fiction could benefit from a character growth arc rooted in an emotional wound. A character has a reasonable misbelief about the world, like "I can't trust anyone" based on a childhood experience of being tricked by a best friend, or "people always leave me" based on being abandoned by a parent. Real people have damage—so should your characters. Give readers enough backstory to understand what holds the character back. The character will need to challenge and confront their misbelief throughout the story in an internal story arc, with steps forward and backward as events challenge but later reinforce their misbelief. Eventually, they learn and grow and their outlook on the world is changed.

Recommendations:

- *Writing the Intimate Character* by Jordan Rosenfeld

- *The Emotional Craft of Fiction* by Donald Maass

- *Creating Character Arcs* (and the related workbook) by K.M. Weiland

- *The Emotional Wound Thesaurus* by Ackerman & Puglisi

GMC plus stakes: This fundamental concept in fiction writing means that readers should be able to determine the main character's goal (what they want), their motivation (why they want it), and the conflict (what stands in the main character's way, what they will need to overcome to achieve their goal). A related concept is stakes (what will happen/what will the main character or others lose if the main character fails to meet their goal). When

I read a WIP that lacks sufficient GMC, it often reads more like a diary than a story.

Here's an example:

> Hector got up in the morning and fed the animals in the shelter. He drove to town and bought supplies but had to go to three different places because he couldn't get Rodent Chow at his usual store. He bought a lottery ticket. He returned home and watched the news and the lottery drawing. His numbers didn't win.

This is plot, a listing of everything that happens. Hector has something resembling goals—animal care, shopping, and watching TV. But there is no motivation and no reason why anyone would care. And even when there is a bit of conflict (no Rodent Chow at the Farm and Barn store), that conflict is resolved quickly and with no real impact on the main character. There are no stakes, no consequences. I got bored writing it.

But what if we injected GMC and stakes into Hector's day?

> Hector scraped the last serving of Rodent Chow into the trough. He couldn't wait any

longer for Farm and Barn to notify him that his order was ready—his animals would be hungry again tonight. He was the only one protecting the thirty-five animals in his charge, rodents who'd been injured or missed necessary socialization skills—unlikely to survive in the wild. He grabbed his reusable shopping bags and headed to town in his pickup.

When he got to Farm and Barn, a sign was posted on the register: "We no longer carry Rodent Chow." Well dag-nabbit. Nice of them to tell him. Ever since Mayor Sally and her angry mob showed up at his farm, complaining about a small hole in the fence he hadn't yet had a chance to repair, he was persona non grata in Crow Wing County. But he couldn't just pull up stakes and move—where else could they go? He'd spent everything on the down payment for the farm. Even if he could sell it, he'd take a loss in closing costs and not have the funds to buy a place with enough land elsewhere.

He struck out at the hardware store too, and eventually ended up at the grocery store, buying expensive people food that he knew his animals could eat. This was crushing his savings, and he'd yet to get any customers to his online store selling Hector's Haven apparel and merchandise. At the register, he saw the lottery kiosk and the six million dollar current payout. He bought a ticket, opting for ramen rather than a burger tonight for himself—again. This ticket could be his saving grace. If only something would go his way.

The local news carried stories about the weather and the impact of the drought on the sweet corn crop. But sure, all the blame for Klein's sad harvest fell on two of his weasels eating a total of six ears of corn—so unfair. The lottery drawing was next. Hector crossed his fingers. *Well, shoot.* He didn't match a single number.

In the first example, I feel nothing for Hector. He's generic and having a dull day. But in the second, we're along for the ride with Hector on his emotional roller coaster of a day. We know what he wants (even if it isn't earth-changing) and we know why (protecting vulnerable rodents from being released into the wild). Knowing Hector's GMC changes how readers view the events, the plot that "happens," because we know how it impacts a character who—if drawn well—has become a person we care about. The definitive craft book on GMC is *Goal, Motivation, and Conflict* by Debra Dixon.

Worldbuilding/Setting: This concept can be more than giving your characters a cool place to hang out. Worldbuilding done right can make the setting an integral part of the story. I've read manuscripts that could be set in a cloud, and unless it's an off-world scene from *Good Omens* with Aziraphale covering for Crowley, it usually leaves me feeling that the story is lacking something. As a reader, it's a missed opportunity—I want to know where and when this story is taking place and that the setting matters. For contemporary stories, authors can sometimes get away with having something occurring vaguely "now" and vaguely "in our world," but even if your setting is a fictional town in an unnamed state (like Springfield is for both *The Simpsons* and *Guiding Light*), give that setting parameters. How big is it? What are the primary industries? Does everyone know each other? How close are they to needed resources? Is everyone attending the same high school, or are there two rival schools? Whatever is important to your characters, make it clear, consistent, and realistic in your setting. Even in high fantasy with a city built on a floating island filled with magical creatures, the rules of the universe need to be consistent and clear. If some characters can fly but others can't, give a reason. If gravity works backward, how does that impact everything? (I do not recommend this unless you're Lionel Ritchie, dancing on the ceiling.)

Our goal for setting in Step Two is making sure:

1. There is a setting

2. It's clear and consistent, internally logical, and matches your genre

3. The setting works in service of the story

That's it. Step Two is long enough. Confirm the setting is not interfering with the plot and other big-picture issues.

But don't fret, fans of worldbuilding—we'll be back at it again in greater detail in Step Three.

My favorite books on setting and worldbuilding are:

- *A Writer's Guide to Active Setting* by Mary

Buckham (applies to all genres)

- *Wonderbook* by Jeff VanderMeer (aimed more at speculative fiction, fantasy, and sci-fi)

Genre Norms: This is more important if you are pursuing traditional publishing than if you plan to go with indie publishing, but it's smart to be aware of reader expectations. Romance readers will be justifiably upset if the novel that you are pitching as a romance ends with the characters apart, alone, or dead. A "happy ever after" ending (or at least a "happy for now" ending) is a genre expectation. Don't think readers will praise you for innovation—they'll run you out of Romancelandia on a rail (well, with bad reviews warning other romance fans off). Readers looking for their genre don't have time to waste on genre-busters. Mystery readers want that mystery solved with all the clues available by the end of the story. Sci-fi readers want a scientific basis for the not-yet-available advances in tech and changes in the world. They won't be satisfied with an "it's magic" explanation. It's not innovative or cute to refuse to follow (or to be unaware of) genre norms. It's breaking the promise you made to your readers when you said your story was a romance, or a mystery, or a sci-fi, or whatever genre. Don't be that author.

Take a look at your story. Read through the manuscript, thinking about whether the story "holds together" now.

Sure, there are still things you can do to make this better written, but the story should be solid, and the plot coherent, the characters acting reasonably and in pursuit of their goals, which are known and logical. We're hoping to hear "of course" rather than "huh?" when we get feedback from critique partners and beta readers in Step Four.

Once you finish revising for these big picture issues, this is your **Draft Two – which is all about story structure/arcs.** Celebrate completing Draft Two and Step Two, perhaps with a two-step.

The Bonus Content for this chapter is "do not disturb" door hanger downloads. If you can get bond paper or tape/glue it to some thin cardboard, all the better. This would be the perfect use for my laminator. There are three designs: one for Plotters, Pantsers, and Plantsers (which is someone whose method is in-between plotting and pantsing).

> ## Bonus Content: Don't Disturb the Writer door hangers

Do Not Disturb
Writing in Progress

I'M A PLOTTER

Don't make me plot your demise in my next manuscript!

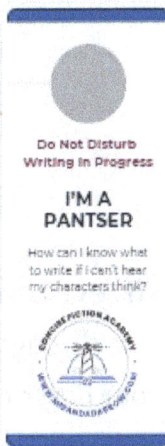

Do Not Disturb
Writing in Progress

I'M A PANTSER

How can I know what to write if I can't hear my characters think?

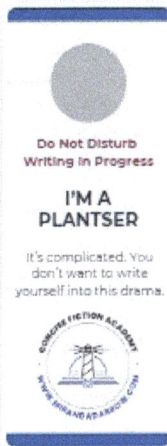

Do Not Disturb
Writing in Progress

I'M A PLANTSER

It's complicated. You don't want to write yourself into this drama.

1 - Plotter 2 - Pantser 3 - Plantser

Step Three

Add Depth

I n this step, you'll revise for paragraph-level
changes. This time through the document, the
goal is to improve your description of setting, add
snappier dialogue, and work on showing instead of
telling. You'll make sure you're ending your scenes
with the best possible hooks that don't bury your
dialogue in the middle of long paragraphs and
add more "oomph" to your pages. This is where
your author voice comes alive and where you add

nuances to your scenes. This round of revisions will result in your Draft Three.

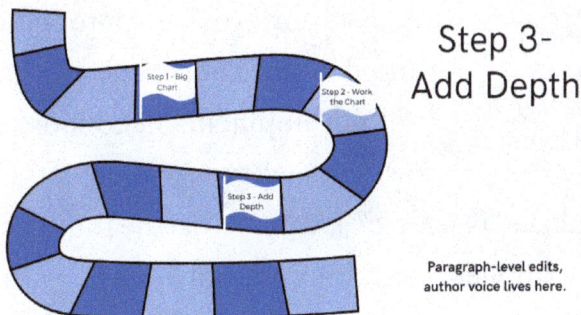

Step 3-
Add Depth

Step 1 - Big Chart

Step 2 - Work the Chart

Step 3 - Add Depth

Paragraph-level edits, author voice lives here.

First let's check in with our Revision Roadmap, which shows us working through seemingly "unnecessary" twists when a straight line diagonally across the board is more direct. Like much of life, revisions are about the journey. Those extra miles are the hard work our readers deserve because they help us get to the best possible version of our manuscript.

Foreshadowing: You largely worked out your plot issues in Step Two, but here's an opportunity to make sure you've appropriately buried hints and clues. Do your plot developments need more (or less) foreshadowing? Your plot twist should be "of course" and not "what the fruitcake?!"

Booker is watching for foreshadowing.

This applies especially to any story with a mystery plot or subplot, but *all* novels need foreshadowing—hints lying in plain sight that don't draw a lot of attention to themselves at first glance. Then, after the secret is revealed or the mystery is solved, readers can go, "Oh yeah, I remember." They may even flip back through the pages (or scroll back, or rewind) to find where you had buried that clue but obfuscated it by misdirection. Don't mind this Chekov's gun sitting here on the coffee table. Let's watch this marching band stomping through our scene, breaking Granny's tea set instead.

Unless your WIP is a soap opera, the "answer" to the story question shouldn't be a main character's evil twin no one acknowledged existed until the final chapter. The "solution" to a tricky problem that has stumped the protagonist should not be a *deus ex machina* element that shows up to fix everything. Readers deserve fair storytelling and will feel cheated if the answer to the story's question doesn't have a solid textual basis. Readers won't be entertained by Sherlock noticing something back in chapter one that was never mentioned because POV character Watson was too "not-Sherlock" to notice and comment upon it. Don't make your POV character an unintentionally unreliable narrator by not wanting to "spoil" the book by giving readers the clues. Give them and hide them in plain sight.

Promise to the readers: Another common error is writers trying to make their first pages ultra-exciting to grab readers but the rest of the book is quiet and introspective, resulting in a complete mismatch. This happens frequently with prologues featuring other characters or an earlier timeline—something exciting happens and then—we never see them again. I'm not saying that all prologues are bad. Most are unnecessary and delay readers from bonding with your main character. If the information in your prologue is crucial, consider whether there's a later point to bring it in while keeping the spotlight on your protagonist in the opening pages. You want to appeal to the reader who will like your entire book, not just the first chapter, so keep your promise from the first pages and don't pull a "bait and switch" stunt on potential readers.

- Do not leave plot threads hanging.

- The clues and suspects need to be visible—you don't want surprise or out-of-the-blue solutions.

- Follow genre norms if you are promoting your book as a specific genre.

- Match the story tone and style to the cover copy and first pages.

Setting and worldbuilding, part two: In Step Two, our charge was to make sure you *have* a setting and that it's logical and internally coherent so that it doesn't interfere with the story's big picture.

Now we're digging deeper into worldbuilding:

- Are there "info-dumping" passages?

- Are there opportunities to weave necessary backstory into the action of the scene?

- Are you filtering the setting through the POV character's perspective?

- How many senses are invoked with your descriptions?

If you have a close POV (first or close third), the details describing the setting should be how the POV character views the scene. A character likely won't comment on their home community unless something has changed. If your POV character is new to the area, everything is fresh and interesting. It's natural for readers to explore the setting along with the newcomer POV character. However, if your POV character has lived in the same small community their whole life, not much catches their attention unless it's shiny and new. A classic example: Netherfield Park has been let at last!

Your descriptions of the setting should include more than visual cues: don't forget to describe the sounds, smells, tastes, and how things feel (the squishiness of the carpet, sharp grass cutting your wet shins). Bring that scenery to life so readers can be transported into that world. But just a pinch—don't bore them to tears by describing every blade of grass. Focus on the parts that interest your unique POV character.

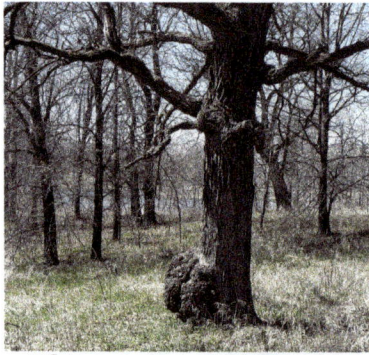

*This tree reminded me of
Christopher Meloni.*

Characters will notice what has changed, what is "off," or what is out of place. They shouldn't describe their home like they're auditioning for a show on HGTV unless their futon is on fire or suddenly and inexplicably missing. The setting details selected say as much about the POV character as it does the setting, so deepen your POV and develop character nuance by filtering those details through the POV character's lens. The photos I include in this book paint a picture of me and my viewpoint.

Fantasy, sci-fi, and historical novels need setting as an essential genre element. But readers do not need every detail of your story's universe. Sift through and pick out the important details. Don't include every element of your worldbuilding in the manuscript, such as the grammatical details of all the languages that you created for groups of characters. Save that for later books, your website, or newsletter bonuses. Please don't info-dump that onto your readers to impress readers with your thoroughness—they are reading fiction for a story with a plot, not just worldbuilding.

Instead of putting every detail on the page, consider creating a story universe bible: a place to house your worldbuilding details in a separate document. Pull that up whenever you add another detail to retain continuity.

Tips for revising to enhance your story's setting:

- Selecting the right level of specificity and picking which setting details to include is an ongoing process.

- You may need to condense excess details and make your descriptions concise.

- Pick details that are important to your POV

or main character—which also ties into character development and deepening the POV.

- High-quality setting descriptions can be an opportunity for foreshadowing and symbolism.

A word about dialogue and character voice: There's plenty to say about dialogue. My favorite writing craft books are James Scott Bell's *How to Write Dazzling Dialogue: The Fastest Way to Improve Any Manuscript* and the Writer's Digest anthology *Crafting Dynamic Dialogue: The Complete Guide to Speaking, Conversing, Arguing, and Thinking in Fiction.*

Here are some tips for making your dialogue sing:

- Give "voice" to each character by reading the dialogue aloud (or having your computer read it to you).

- Select words that fit each character's

background.

- Trim unnecessary details, like "Hello, how's your mom?" and long goodbyes (tough for Midwesterners).

- Avoid long monologues, Hamlet.

- Don't "bury" your dialogue in long paragraphs that start and end with narrative text.

Word choice in dialogue is key for character voice—consider the character's level of education, experience, and worldview. Does each key character's "voice" sound distinct? Whose dialogue passages always take up a full paragraph, and which character rarely says anything more than "Yup" or "Nope." Do you have a character who sees the world through a musical lens, one who would describe the short burst of gunfire as staccato and the rising drama as a crescendo?

For example, think about how a typical lawyer talks, thinks, and draws analogies. It's not the same way that a doctor, a landscaper, a young child, or an alien from a distant universe arriving on Earth for the first time would likely describe the world. How does each character talk and think? How do they compare things (analogies, metaphors, and similes)? To enhance character voice, make character cheat sheets for all your main characters that track their worldview, frame of reference, interests, etc. See below for a template in this section's Bonus Content.

If your beta readers and/or critique partners think your characters are too similar or generic, make sure the characters' names aren't too similar, as that can confuse readers. List your characters alphabetically by first name. See if they start with the same first letter or sound alike. Make sure you don't have three characters named Chris (which I don't recommend unless you're writing Marvel Universe fanfic that breaks the fourth wall, in which case, carry on).

If a character has a catchphrase, reserve its use for just that one character, unless it's a plot point that they are an influencer and their unique phrase is catching on among their friend group. Sometimes it's more interesting if "Fetch" is just not going to happen, Gretchen.

Identify clunky "As you know, Bob" dialogue where one character tells another something they both already know. For example: "We're here because of the government decree made by my uncle, the King, who was responsible for the death of your son, Francis, who had been my betrothed...." This is a form of info-dumping and annoys readers.

Having the dialogue be 100% realistic is *not* the goal. We want compelling. Cut the clutter. Real-life conversations are often dull, sorry to say. I'm a practicing attorney and I've edited books by and about attorneys. Almost always, it's better to select words to show authenticity like subpoena and *voir dire*—words readers would associate with attorneys, rather than subject poor readers to actual legal text: "Whereas, the party of the first part hereby . . ." Fiction readers are looking for an escape, not a punishment.

A mentor told me to let my dialogue shine on the page by starting and/or ending the paragraph with it. You can include dialogue tags, action beats, or even narrative text between dialogue or on *one* end of that paragraph, but not both. Readers' eyes gravitate toward dialogue passages. They can get skipped if they're the lettuce or cheese in your narrative text sandwich of a paragraph.

Show, Don't Tell (the short version): This is a topic for an entire writing craft book, including Janice Hardy's *Understanding Show, Don't Tell (And Really Getting It).* For Step Three, we're focused on two situations to show, rather than tell, readers.

SDT for character emotions: Avoid naming emotions, especially for POV characters, if you can convey them without resorting to emotional pantomime. Yes, sometimes writers go a bit too far and we're left shrugging and swallowing the lump in our throat and tugging at our collar, wondering what emotion the author is trying to convey. But at least those authors are trying to let the reader figure it out rather than spray-painting the character's emotions all over the text.

*This squirrel staring me
down. The nerve!*

There are many squirrels where I live in central Minnesota. One made a nest under the hood of my car and tore up the insulation for bedding—big mess. My husband attempted to evict him with a bar of Irish Spring soap and then some spicy garlic and jalapeño sauce that he'd found on the internet as a natural repellant. The squirrels weren't leaving. For weeks, I had to slam on my hood to get them out before I started my car. The whole time my car smelled like old dudes hanging out at the Olive Garden after showering. The squirrels eventually left. Do I need to tell you how I feel about them, or have I shown it sufficiently with this rant?

Character emotions and how your main character feels about what's happening are best conveyed through their dialogue and actions, rather than "telling" readers in the narrative text. "Sue was sad." A more effective way to do this is to describe how we *know* Sue is sad by observing her. One of my favorite writing craft resources is *The Emotion Thesaurus* by Angela Ackerman and Becca Puglisi. It's a helpful guide with lots of alternatives for showing the character's emotions through their visceral reactions and outward appearance, rather than naming the emotion.

Another issue is when the author both shows *and* tells readers the character's emotions. If the dialogue and character's actions have already made that character's feelings clear, it's unnecessary (and unwanted) to also name that emotion. Readers may feel you don't trust them to follow the clues. Readers like figuring it out.

 **SDT key events and dialogue, don't summarize:** In Step Two, I recommended that authors show, don't tell, scenes with key events in the story timeline when we were searching for "missing scenes." If you see a key

event being summarized, consider showing it "live." One story I read starts with a group of soldiers gathered around a battlefield gossiping about all the bad-ass things their leader (the main character) had just done. We care less about these looky-loos than our hero. Let's see that scene, live on the page, from the main character's perspective. What are they feeling and thinking as this battle unfolds? What is their goal—to win, or just to survive? Don't skip this immersive and pivotal scene.

Similarly, if you find a passage summarizing a conversation between two characters who are in the scene, show that dialogue rather than tell a summary of the conversation. An exception is if readers have already seen this event or explanation and this scene is needed for getting another character up to speed. Using real dialogue is more interesting than a summary, as it gives the characters' voices.

Here's an example:

Summarized dialogue:
- Sally told Hector about the importance of the Sweet Corn Days festival and its impact on the city budget.

Actual dialogue:

- Sally pointed at the hole in the fence. "If Farmer Klein's sweet corn crop is destroyed, we'll have nothing to serve at next week's Sweet Corn Days festival. It's the top tourist event all year. The city relies on it for half of our budget. We won't be able to fix the water tower if we have to cancel the festival."

The longer you write, the more you develop the skills to recognize Show, Don't Tell, to be mindful of setting, and to be more character-specific in your dialogue. Experienced writers may have little to revise here. But some authors always need to add more, like those with sparse settings or who forget to put transitions between the POV shifts. Full employment for editors, that's what I call that. *Wink!*

When you finish revising the full manuscript for paragraph-level issues, you have completed Draft Three (out of four, you're almost there) and it's time to celebrate! We are now halfway through the Six Steps, and I admit

these are the hardest steps. This Worldbuilding Checklist is short and applies to any genre. You can find long checklists that outline elements of your fantasy or sci-fi universe. I've also included the Character Worksheet mentioned above.

Bonus Content: Worldbuilding Checklist & Character Worksheet

BOOK MD EDITING
by Miranda Darrow

Six-Step Revision Process
Worldbuilding Checklist:

- Ground readers in the time (season, hour) and place
- Avoid cliché settings and watch for info-dumping
- Filter the description of setting through the POV character:
  - Pick details they'd notice
  - Use more than one sense to make the setting more immersive for readers
- Integrate setting details into the story action, let readers see the world in use
- Be clear, consistent, and logical within your world's parameters

Get your worldbuilding in ship-shape

www.mirandadarrow.com

Character Worksheet

Name:

Age:

Occupation:

Education Level:

Field of Study:

Hobbies:

Family of Origin:

Relationship Status:

Any Children:

Personality Type:

Other Unique Features:

Step Four

Get Feedback and Incorporate

Step Four involves getting feedback from critique partners and/or beta readers. Step Four is interesting because it can often take the longest, but it involves a fair amount of waiting and *not* working on your manuscript. To me, this is one of the easiest steps. That's only been the case since I've found a trusted group of critique partners. I'll help you do that in this chapter if you haven't already found your writing pals. Pick wisely, because how much you enjoy this step is directly related to how much you enjoy reading the WIPs of your critique partners.

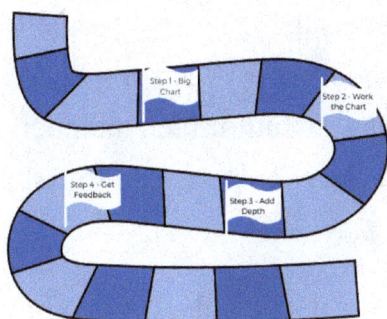

Step 4- Feedback

Get eyes on your pages, (CP and/or BR) & incorporate.

Now is a good time to get eyes on your manuscript. Let's talk terminology first, since writers throw around the terms "critique partners" and "beta readers" (and sometimes "alpha readers.") Who are these people?

- Critique Partners are fellow writers who will read part or all of your manuscript and give feedback on the story. They often know a fair amount about story structure and craft because they are also writers. This service is usually provided at no cost and in exchange for you reading and critiquing a portion or all of their manuscript.

- Beta Readers are readers who are not usually writers. They will read a portion or all of your manuscript and give (hopefully honest) feedback. They know less about the craft of writing than most writers do. These folks are often super-readers (people who read tons of books every year) or specifically fans of you as an author (i.e., members of your author Facebook page and/or street team).

- For example, a Beta Reader may comment that they had a hard time "connecting" with the main character. A Critique Partner is more likely to be able to articulate what exactly the writing craft problem is that's causing a disconnect with the main character, whether they lack a clear GMC, came off as heartless and failed to "Save the Cat," or if they simply don't like characters named Eugene because they had an ex named that (in which case, carry on).

- Alpha Readers are readers (not necessarily authors) who read a draft or parts of your manuscript before you attempt to revise, usually earlier than Step Four. They are the "first" person besides the author to read any portion of the story. Not all authors use alpha readers, and I didn't include them in my Six Steps because I haven't imposed my earliest drafts on anyone.

This is a part of my presentation where I usually get questions. Sometimes, I don't even have to bribe friends to show up and ask.

Which are better: CPs or BRs?

My answer: CPs are more valuable for several reasons:

- They give more specific and actionable feedback.

- They have a built-in incentive to keep the details and text of your manuscript confidential because you also have *their* manuscript.

- Being a CP for other writers and identifying writing issues for them can teach you so much about story structure, improve your writing, and help you be a better self-editor.

- CPs can be your writing pals who commiserate with you through the query trenches, cheer you on with your successes, and form your circle of friends who really "get" what you're going through as a writer. My CPs have become close friends, more than any relationship I've had with a BR. Your best shot of getting mentioned in someone's acknowledgments page is being their CP, and being the author's romantic partner is probably your second best bet.

Are CPs or BRs going to steal my book and publish it themselves?

My answer:

- It's possible but unlikely.

- Yes, there are awful people out there who steal books. Vet your readers before you send anyone a full manuscript. A reputable publishing professional such as an agent or editor is much less likely to breach confidentiality because they have their professional reputation and livelihood on the line.

- Whether you should file for a copyright for your manuscript is a topic beyond the scope of this craft book. That is one way to prove you are the original author if someone attempts to steal and publish your manuscript.

> Do I really need to get feedback from someone else?

My answer is:

- Really, yes.

- If you aren't an experienced writer sending your latest manuscript to your agent, you need someone to read your stuff before you send it out to agents or upload it on Kindle Direct. Unless you are truly writing for your personal amusement or for "family legacy" and don't intend to inflict your novel on the general public, for the sake of everyone's eyeballs, please get some feedback.

- I'm a professional editor. I've been writing for decades. I hired another editor to edit this book on writing craft advice even though it's based on presentations I've given many times and on a topic I know intimately. Why would I do that, when I'm so unquestionably fabulous? Because our mind fills in the information we already "know" about the story when we read, skipping right over duplicate words, glaring plot holes, and using two different names for the same character unintentionally (true story).

- We know our own story too well, so none of these problems stand out to us. We need someone not in our head to do it. Some authors swear the Microsoft Word Read Aloud feature helps, since it's not your eyes. I can see how this might be helpful for copyediting issues, such as spotting missed and duplicate words (though homonyms, not so much). But Siri and Alexa can't point out your character's flagging motivation and missing key scenes.

What feedback can I get from BRs?

My answer:

- These are readers, not necessarily writers. If they're good BRs, they can point to what's working but may not be able to articulate areas that need improvement.

- For example, they don't like X character—but why? Are they able to articulate that X lacks agency? Lacks GMC? Lacks decency?

- Concepts like pacing, proportion, plot holes, and POV head-hopping may annoy BRs but they may not identify/name the problem.

- They help find out what's working and gauge reader reactions.

> What if I don't want to read anyone else's terrible manuscript?

My answer, having never received quite such a blunt condemnation of fellow authors while at a writing conference (I can't imagine that would go over swimmingly) is:

- Money can solve this problem. Of course it can. You can hire professional BRs and/or a freelance editor.

- A professional will read it within the

contracted timeframe and will not expect you to read anything in exchange.

> Should I give my CP or BR a list of questions?

My answer: It's helpful, especially if someone is new to giving feedback. For the Bonus Content for Step Four, I have a list of questions you can ask your critique partners or beta readers about your WIP.

Where do you find critique partners and/or beta readers? BRs are often people you know—friends and family members who like to read, coworkers whom you know to be readers, people from your book club(s) if your book club actually reads the book and doesn't just gossip and drink wine. Ideally, BRs are readers of your genre in your target demographic, such as teenagers if you're writing YA.

There are professional BR organizations, including The Spun Yarn and The Darling Axe, agencies that charge a fee and pay the BRs. My seventeen-year-old son has been a beta reader through one of these sites for four years and enjoys getting paid to read books. The BRs fill out a survey with pre-set questions about character and plot. The authors can add a few additional questions. These organizations match authors with readers in their target demographic.

Your best sources for CPs are writing groups (local or online) where you have gotten to know the other author and think that they are a reasonable person who could give good feedback. If you don't have a writers' group (or if no one in the group is open to a CP swap, writing your genre, etc.) there are places you can look, mostly online. If you are already a published author and you've picked up this book because you're trying to get more organized and methodical with your revisions, then you've come to the right place. You have more options for BRs. Ask your street team, Facebook group, etc. Readers love free books and having a sneak peek. But remind them to keep the text confidential, as there have been issues of high-profile leaks (see Stephenie Meyer's fiasco from nearly twenty years ago).

How many CPs and/or BRs should you get for Step Four? Your needs may vary. I aim for four to five, sometimes more.

Here are some places you can find critique partners.

- Savvy Authors (free events)

- Twitter/X events like #CPMatch (see below for my fabulous results)

- KM Weiland's "Helping Writers Become Authors" website

- Facebook/Meta groups including:

  ○ The Writing Gals

  ○ Alessandra Torres Inkers

  ○ 20BooksTo50K

- Critique groups for members of larger writing groups:

  ○ Women's Fiction Writing Association (WFWA)

  ○ Sisters-in-Crime (online or local chapters)

- ○ SFWA (Sci-Fi)

- ○ SCBWI (kid-lit)

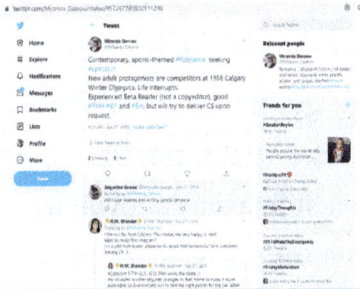

My Tweet from 2018 in a #CPMatch event where I met 3 awesome CPs.

Vetting potential CPs and BRs. Now you've found some CP and/or BR and it's time to vet your readers. It's best if the writer is writing in your genre (or reader enjoys your genre). If that isn't possible, make sure they are at least familiar with your genre and won't drag you for things that are genre expectations. Don't toss your whole manuscript at them right away, though. Have some chill—swap three chapters or fifty pages or something that is "meaty" enough to get past your already hyper-edited first pages and into the heart of the story where things might go off the rails.

Do one or two rounds of feedback and see if you and the other author click. If so, set a schedule with dates for getting comments back that works for both parties. Usually, newer authors are overly protective, but still make sure you trust this person with your manuscript and that you are getting value from their feedback. Make sure that the feedback they give you is actionable and specific and can help you learn and grow as a writer.

Evaluating feedback: So you're exchanging pages and getting feedback or hiring someone to give you feedback. That takes time. And no one wants you messing around in the document while they're reading it, so put it down and walk away. It's good to take a break so you'll be fresh when you revise the next time. While you're waiting to hear back, you can jump ahead to Step Six and start working on that set of tasks. As you write and revise more manuscripts, collect reliable CPs and/or BRs and protect them like the treasures they are.

Exchanging feedback with other writers or readers takes time, but getting at least three other opinions allows patterns to emerge. You might dismiss one person's opinion that your main character is a Mary Sue with no character arc. But if you hear that same critique from multiple sources, it's something you need to consider. As a writer, I get conflicting feedback too. I recently entered a flash fiction contest and received both kudos and rotten tomatoes from the various judges on the exact same parts of my story. This 1,000 word flash fiction featured siblings of an influencer couple and parodied influencer culture.

What I liked about the story:

This is a creative take on the monster-people that social media has created! This line in particular:"You're harshing our content-creation vibe," said one of Caitlyn's girl gang. "We've mood-boarded Clark and Ana in tuxedos serving their sibs cake and champagne." cracked me up. Both "vibe" and "mood boarding" are definitely 2024 speak, very now, and they make we want to delete my instagram and throw my phone off a bridge.

This story also accomplishes a LOT in a very compact space. Through use of clever dialogue ("you aren't being a supportive Dude of Honor"!) amd description ("The sky snapped and sparkled through the moon roof"), the story has a distinct modern feel.

This contest judge liked my use of 2024 influencer speak.

> I found a number of the sentences a struggle to read. For example, what was going on in the scene below? I feel that a "show not tell" approach would have worked better. I also struggled with the word choice 'harshing' it did not seem like something the character would say and I wondered why it was in the sentence, as it broke up the flow.
>
> "You're harshing our content-creation vibe," said one of Caitlyn's girl gang. "We've mood-boarded Clark and Ana in tuxedos serving their sibs cake and champagne."
>
> Another example was this sentence without context. "At least no followers are crashing the wedding," Clark said.
>
> Were either of the couple or the guests celebrities? If not, why would followers crash the weather. If it was Caitlyns 4th wedding, then perhaps they were not teenagers or early twenties. Also the location of a mountain cabin made it seem quite remote. That sentence did not add anything to the story.

This judge didn't care for my influencer speak.

What do you do with conflicting feedback? Consider whether the reader is in your target market. Is the feedback coming from more than one reader who knows your genre and whose tastes aren't the polar opposite of your own?

You can ignore one person's opinion that doesn't match your vision for your story. This is *your* manuscript. Follow your vision for it. However, if you get multiple CPs or BRs raising the same issue, it is something you should address.

When to seek an outside opinion:

- When someone raises a serious red flag, indicating that you may need an authenticity reader.

- When multiple CPs spot the same issue.

- When you don't agree—or you agree but don't know how to address the concern in a way that satisfies you and your readers.

- When you feel like your story is still missing something but you can't identify it.

I'm often the mediator between an author and their CPs when the author wants an outside opinion about whether a subplot is working, or whether a major developmental editing change is needed (such as changing POV or eliminating or adding a POV character, changing the ending, eliminating a major subplot, etc.). With an outside perspective, I can often help the author find a solution that works for them and addresses comments from their CPs. Pacing issues, missed story beats, and characters acting inconsistently with their stated GMC can all benefit from fresh eyes. If there are still big-picture concerns, work this out before moving on to line edits.

Incorporating feedback: After resolving any issues about whether the feedback is valid, get to work. If necessary, pull out your Big Chart and figure out how and where to implement this big-picture edit, and then do a quick second-round pass of the changed text. Using track changes and version comparison tools in Word can save you a lot of wasted time and effort.

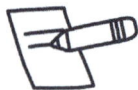

We're finally touching your manuscript again!

Some writers dive in to incorporate their feedback as soon as they get it. Others treat this as a single pass by gathering up all their feedback, placing it in order, then working through the full WIP. There's room in-between for all sorts of chaos. I've grouped this process together as part of Step Four but acknowledge it might be multiple rounds during Step Four, one big sweep at the end of Step Four, or you (being a rebel) could tackle the incorporation of feedback into Step Five at the same time you are focusing on line-level edits. It's all good. Do what works for you.

For the Bonus Content for Step Four, I have a list of questions you can ask your CPs or BRs about your WIP. CPs are more likely to know writing concepts, so adapt this as you see fit. It's a good starting point and not an overwhelming number of questions to foist onto the volunteers you have lined up.

Bonus Content: Beta Reader/Critique Partner Questionnaire

BOOK MD EDITING

Questions to ask Beta Readers and/or Critique Partners:

- Does the premise grab your attention and offer an original angle?
- Is the plot well-developed and plausible?
- Can you identify the main character and their goal, motivation, and conflict?
- Are the stakes clear?
- Is the obstacle that stands in the protagonist's way of reaching their goal clear?
- Has the writer either laid out or hinted at a clear story question in this opening and conveyed a sense that not all is well in the protagonist's world?
- Were you successfully oriented in the novel's time and space (setting)?
- Is the information about the characters and setting sprinkled in organically (instead of info-dumps)?
- Are the characters interesting, complex, and authentic?
- Were there any main characters who didn't feel real to you, or that you didn't feel a connection to? Which ones? Why?
- Were there any parts that felt unrealistic to you?
- Is the dialogue believable and well-crafted?
- Were there places that jarred you or pulled you out of the story? Which part(s) and why?
- Anywhere you felt disengaged, confused, or impatient to get to more action?
- Did the story hold together and feel complete?
- Was the end satisfying?
- Anything else you would like to tell me about the story so I can improve it?

Step Five

Line Edits

Line-level revisions make your prose sparkle! It's time to take one more look through the full manuscript and revise for sentence-level issues. This includes using more active verbs and active voice, matching narrative text to the characters, mastering dialogue mechanics, and copyediting. Line-level revisions contain multiple topics worthy of their own books.

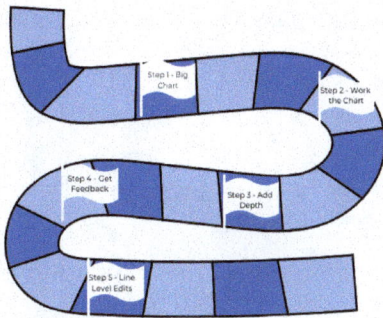

Step 5-
Line Edits

Dig into your sentence
structure and word choice
to make your prose sparkle!

Active Voice: Identify and replace some (not necessarily all) of your sentences that contain passive voice. Too many passive-voice passages result in dull writing. There is a time and place for passive voice. That time is in dusty legal prose where no one wants to "take credit" for an action, so we remove the subject and let the action be something that "happened" without a named actor/person doing it. For example: "The items were removed from the premises on January 15th between the hours of 10 p.m. and 2 a.m." By whom? We don't know. And that's often the point—we don't know but need to find out. It's intentionally passive voice because we either don't know or we are being coy and refuse to name the person (or creature) responsible for removing the items.

Tip: if you can logically end the sentence with "by zombies," it's in the passive voice and missing a subject.

For example:

- Farmer Klein's cornfield was invaded.

- Farmer Klein's cornfield was invaded by zombies!

In the first one, we don't know who or what invaded the field. Maybe Hector's weasels were wrongly accused.

There are other valid uses (being cryptic and evasive key among them), but for most fiction, active voice is stronger and more engaging. You could have a character who speaks predominantly in passive voice, but if it's every character, that would bog the story down.

Booker leaping into action.

Active Verbs: Similar to active voice, using active verbs in your sentences packs more punch than passive verbs/linking verbs (or even generic active verbs). Multiple sentences in a paragraph that describe how a person looks or their job function, a veritable linking verbs-a-palooza? That's a snoozefest. This is also why so many descriptions of settings get flagged as info-dumping, if they're a laundry list describing the setting but no *action* is taking place. Action verbs were featured in the *Schoolhouse Rock* episode/song "Verb: It's What's Happening!"

Terminology check:

- **Active verbs** show the action of the sentence, the subject DOES something: He RAN. She JUMPED. We all SCREAM for ice cream. This includes most verbs.

- **Passive verbs** (also called **linking verbs**) show status or define the subject/noun of the sentence) but they don't "do" anything. Examples:

  ○ all versions of the verb "to be" (am, is, are,

was, were, be, being, been)

- ○ other "status" verbs such as: appear, feel, become, grow, look, seem, remain, smell, sound, stay, taste

Many of these status verbs can be either linking or action, depending on whether the sentence is **describing/defining** the subject or if the subject is actually **doing** something.

For example:

- Pepper smells clean after her bath. [Here "smell" is a linking verb, describing Pepper and her aroma.]

- Pepper smells the goose poop and then eats it. [Here "smell" is an action verb, as she's engaging her nose to savor the scent as she decides to gobble down goose guano.]

Overuse of "boring" active verbs (like "make" and "do") which are common can render your prose generic and uninspiring. See what I did there – I replaced "MAKE your prose generic" with "RENDER your prose generic." To me, rendering is more engaging and active than

Booker seeing if he can track down that goose poop.

"making," which is an active verb but a bland one. Bonus points to any rural folks like me who grew up close enough to a rendering plant to flinch every time you see that word because of the smelly memory that word invokes.

How do you find these "strong verbs" to make your sentences dance off the page with energy? A thesaurus or dictionary can help. Enter the bland verb into a free online thesaurus and find similar words. I also use a helpful reference book, *Strong Verbs Strong Voice: A quick reference to improve your writing and impress readers* by Ann Everett. I use it often enough that I've put tabs on the sections I use the most (felt, have, like, walk, etc). Here's a tip: make sure you know what that exciting new verb means, though, as not all synonyms have the same denotations, let alone connotations. A thesaurus-type resource is the first step to more interesting sentences. Making sure your new word fits the context and means what you want to convey are essential next steps. I use my thesaurus to remind me of words I already know and occasionally learn a new word. Like many writers and editors (and people studying for the SAT exam), I have a large vocabulary and almost always find a more interesting verb from the words I already know but which had eluded me while writing.

Sentence length, complexity, variety, and specific uses for long and short sentences.

This is a section about sentence length. All sentences here have exactly seven words. Read these sentences aloud for maximum effect. I tried to do this section with six words. But I could not—I'm too wordy. Imagine reading a whole book like this. It would be a horrible reading experience.

Seriously, try reading the previous paragraph out loud and imagine the audiobook version of that as a novel.

Now imagine the audiobook version of a novel with a different style of narrative, one more flowing and evocative, some might call it purple prose but there isn't anything technically incorrect about it, other than the long and rambling style that reads like a run-on sentence. You might be justifiably concerned about the poor audiobook narrator who needs supplemental oxygen just to be able to make it through a passage, as these sentences go on and on with no end in sight, yet they continue, a literary style to mirror the narrative structure of Cormac McCarthy's *The Road*, where it just keeps going and there aren't any breaks or any chance to rest. Seriously, that novel didn't have any chapters, it just kept going, and I am struggling to remember if it even had scene breaks, but what I remember the most is that we never got the main character's name and I was so darn worn-out when I finished reading it even though it wasn't that long of a book, but it was exhausting, which was an intentional mood. No rest for the unfortunates trying to survive in this apocalypse, a whole meta experience for readers (and that was meta with a lowercase m, predating whatever is happening with that ginormous corporation).

Readability Statistics   ?   ✕

Counts
  Words   213
  Characters   1,008
  Paragraphs   1
  Sentences   4
Averages
  Sentences per Paragraph   4.0
  Words per Sentence   53.2
  Characters per Word   4.6
Readability
  Flesch Reading Ease   24.4
  Flesch-Kincaid Grade Level   23.0
  Passive Sentences   0.0%

                                          OK

Microsoft Word analytic data for my
word salad paragraph.

I entered that passage into Word to calculate the readability stats. This function is available on newer versions of Microsoft Word and I use it to point out when clients are being a bit too wordy, especially that "Words per Sentence" score. Anything over mid-twenties is a bit much. Note though that I wasn't filling it with SAT words because my average characters per word was only 4.6. If challenged, I could get that to ten and toss a fossilized pile of prose your way. Note that Word didn't identify any of these sentences as passive voice. Yay, I have identifiable subjects and active verbs in all *four* sentences in that paragraph. Yes, it was only four sentences—three fewer sentences than in the choppy and odd-sounding "everything is seven words long" paragraph above it.

I was pleased to find I had an Editor Score of 93%. Word labeled it as "formal writing" and the only "error" detected was my use of "meta" because they thought it should be "met." This is why I don't completely trust grammar programs. Meta has been used as a word for decades.

Apologies for talking like my lawyer alter ego.

Neither short nor long sentences are bad, but we need variety. There are times and places in the story for longer, more complex sentences and other places for shorter, staccato prose. So in this section, we'll talk about sentence length, complexity, and the need for variety in several contexts:

- Watching for passages with not enough variety, unless this is intentional to impact the scene's pacing:

- Speed up the pace in high-action scenes by shortening sentence length—make it choppy.

- Slow down in "reflection" scenes with longer more complex sentences, because now it's safe to muse.

• Match the sentence length and complexity to the character.

On a sentence level, pacing is related to sentence length, word choice, and intentionally cutting out quite a bit of narrative text in high-action scenes. Your character is contemplating life in a quiet café when *bam*, a truck crashes into the café, nearly squashing our protagonist. People from the truck jump out and take someone hostage. Here, shift your prose from flowery to direct. Cut your average sentence length to five words or less on average to convey the immediacy of the scene. The fact that there is a single daisy on each table doesn't come into play once the pace speeds up. Your protagonist's focus now is on surviving, getting away, or saving the day, not on interiority (their feelings) or the setting. Throw that character into fight-or-flight mode and write the narrative text and dialogue in a way that demonstrates this urgent pace. Regardless of the genre, you can follow the recommendations for urban fantasy fight scenes with their punchy jabs of dialogue and narrative between breathtaking descriptions of the action of the scene. This is not the time for reflection and observation.

While this is commonly found in action scenes, changing up sentence and paragraph length doesn't require physical action to cause the uptick in pacing. It could be uncovering an important clue, or finding out someone is lying. That scene deserves a faster pace, shorter sentences, and more white space on the page by having each paragraph only a single short line.

Here's an example from Sally and Hector's story, where Sally needs to choose between her duty to the city and her urge to protect Hector, for whom she has growing feelings:

The city council's directions were clear: "Remove that animal sanctuary or you can forget about being mayor." Sally drove to Hector's farm, passing memories of her life in Crow Wing

County at every corner. What would it mean to walk away from public life? To risk the good opinion of everyone she'd ever known? Well, everyone except Hector.

She knocked on Hector's door.

The mink and ermine snuffled in their pen.

What would happen to them if the sanctuary closed?

Still no answer.

Maybe he's not here.

She could post the condemnation notice and run.

He might not know it was her.

But she'd know.

She couldn't face him.

She tucked the condemnation notice into her back pocket and headed toward her truck. Farmer Klein and the rest of the city council could do this without her, even if it cost her the next election. As she started her truck, Hector pulled into the driveway.

Can you feel the seconds tick by as Sally waits on Hector's front step, debating whether to risk her career and community status over what she thinks is right and her relationship with someone she values? The choppy styling lends these sentences a pounding cadence like Sally's nervous heartbeat.

Deeper POV: If you are in your character's (or if multiple POV, characters') head, knowing their thoughts, then you're viewing the story universe through their lens. The narrative text—everything that isn't some other character's dialogue, including descriptions of the setting, the situation, descriptions of other characters—*all* of this is through the POV character's worldview. The goal of deep POV is to picture the setting, the action, the whole story *only* from the perspective of the scene's POV character. Wipe out any commentary from a narrator or directly from the author. Limit the insights to those available to the POV character in that scene.

*Whose perspective? The dog
or the author?*

Don't include information that your POV character doesn't know. Doing so will pull readers out of the story and into literary critic mode. There can be hints about something that they see but don't grasp the significance of until later. It pulls the story out of deep POV when the narrative jumps to the future with lines like "that turned out to be a bad idea." Readers get pulled out of the scene by this disembodied voice of the future, wondering where it originated. Movie trailer guy, is that you? Resist the urge to dump information the POV character has no basis for knowing in this scene. Also, resist intruding into the scene with a narrator or author's voice, unless this is a prominent feature of your story (e.g., an older narrator looking back, like the framework stories in the movies *Stand by Me* and *The Princess Bride*).

Deep POV requires digging into your character. It promotes an active voice by focusing on showing, rather than telling. Editing to deepen your POV includes cutting filter words and reducing to only necessary dialogue tags, since they add distance. Sensory filter words insert (usually unwanted) distance between the character and the reader. If you're writing in Deep POV (either first person or a close third person), strive to have the reader experience the world through the POV character's, eyes, ears, nose, etc. Let the readers actively "see" what the character sees without adding the extra step of telling readers that your POV character is seeing it.

With filters: Sally **felt** an itch and scratched her ankle. She **heard** a strange noise and looked to her left, facing an open field, looking for the source of the noise. Sally l**ooked left and saw** the wide-open valley, and across the expanse, the parking lot for the Circle K. In the parking lot, she **heard** Chuck Mangione playing "Feels So Good." She **thought,** "Now the Sweet Corn Festival is saved!" She **wanted** to tell Hector that his letter-writing campaign worked, but first, she **wanted** to get an autograph.

Without filters: Sally scratched her itchy ankle—those dang nettles. The mournful wail of a flugelhorn interrupted her scratching. She turned toward the noise and searched across the open valley. There, in the Circle K parking lot, surrounded by a throng of tourists snacking on sweet corn and cheese curds, Chuck Mangione played "Feels So Good." The Sweet Corn Festival was saved! She rushed across the field, autograph book and pen in hand. Wait 'til Hector finds out his letter-writing campaign worked!

Remove filters whenever it's possible without changing the meaning or rendering your text confusing. This allows readers to experience the sensations along with your character.

For this step's Bonus Content, I've included a list of common POV filter words that remind readers they are reading (rather than experiencing) the events in the story. Check that out at the end of this chapter.

Punctuating dialogue: We talked about dialogue in Step Three, but learning how to correctly punctuate dialogue is a line-level type of edit. Knowing these few rules will save you (and your copyeditor and/or proofreader) lots of work later. It's not difficult. It just isn't intuitive (like so many grammar rules in English). There are a few quick rules, and then we're on to the next section.

If you are using a dialogue tag, like "said" or "asked," that is considered part of the same sentence as the line of dialogue. As such, use a comma to separate the dialogue from the tag (inside the quotation marks) and treat the dialogue tag part of the sentence as continuing the sentence (no capital letter for the first word in the dialogue tag unless it's a proper noun). If a segment of dialogue starts a sentence, the first letter should be capitalized even if it follows a dialogue tag and comma.

However, if you are using an action beat rather than a dialogue tag, this is considered a separate sentence. End your dialogue with a period and start the action beat sentence with a capital letter.

Each shift of speaker in a conversation starts a new paragraph. Don't "mix" one character's dialogue into the same paragraph as another character's dialogue (or another character's action beat). Here we use short paragraphs, changing every time someone else talks or does something in the scene.

> For example:
> "You pulled it off," an enthused Farmer Klein said. "This could be our best Sweet Corn Days ever."
> He motioned for Sally to join him onstage. "Let's hear from the mayor!"
> "It wasn't just me." An overheated Sally pulled Hector to the podium with her.
> "It was Hector's letter-writing campaign," an overjoyed Sally said, "that saved the day."

Note: this is awful writing, telling rather than showing, but I added unnecessary adjectives to demonstrate the correct use of capital letters. I needed to because Farmer Klein and Sally are both proper nouns. If your line of dialogue ends with an exclamation point or question mark, the only style difference will be the capital letter (or lack thereof). For the dialogue itself, if the quoted text is the start of a sentence, it starts with a capital letter. But if you interrupt the sentence with a dialogue tag, the continued dialogue can start mid-sentence (lowercase unless it's a proper noun.) Once you learn these rules, you can style dialogue correctly while drafting and save yourself a ton of time later. It will make your writing look more polished to agents, acquiring editors, and readers.

Final copyediting tips: This chapter is long, but line edits aren't any more "work" than the previous editing rounds. It's just fussier and less subjective work. This final section is on basic copyediting, which means checking for spelling, grammar, word usage, and punctuation errors. My favorite resource for this is Renni Browne and Dave King's *Self-Editing for Fiction Writers: How to Edit Yourself into Print.*

I have an article on my website about finding "filler" words which often serve no purpose other than cluttering your page. My biggest filler word is "that." I once removed over 1,000 uses of "that" from a 90,000-word manuscript (and still had plenty of "that" to spare). I should probably subtitle my memoir "She's All That" with how much I love tossing that word into every other sentence (usually unnecessarily).

English is littered with the written equivalents of "um" and "uh," which makes for needlessly tedious reading. You don't need to cut all of them. Maybe it's a particular character's quirk that they say "just" in every line of dialogue. But many of these words and phrases can disappear without your prose losing anything except unnecessary words. I have included my list of top filler words and phrases as part of the Bonus Content for this chapter, which you can check out below.

I love using Word's Read Aloud feature for catching missed words, incorrect verb tense, subject/verb agreement issues, etc. Your eyes can "fill in the blanks" and let you see what you intended to say. But Siri and Alexa aren't giving you the benefit of the doubt. These tools are reading what's on the page, making those issues jump out. Hover over the pause button so you can be prepared to dive in and fix those wording issues.

This is the last round of revisions. Make it sparkle! **Celebrate completing Draft Four and Step Five!** I'd say you're done revising your manuscript completely, but that's not likely. Indie authors who do their own manuscript formatting will be staring at PDF proofs before hitting "publish." Traditionally published authors also need to sign off on their proof copies (let alone any revisions the agents and acquiring editors may request along the way). But your WIP is now ready for Step Six, whichever path you follow.

Step Five's Bonus Content is the two-page list of filter, passive, and filler words.

> **Bonus Content: Filler, Passive Verbs, and Filter Word List**

BOOK MD EDITING

Miranda Darrow's Big List of Filter, Filler, and Passive Verbs:

Here's a list of common POV filter verbs that remind readers they are reading (rather than experiencing the events in the story):

- see / saw / notice / noticed / watch / watched
- look / looked
- hear / heard / sound (like) / sounded (like)
- realize / realized / decide / decided
- think / thought / know / knew
- can / should / (to be) able to
- touch / touched / felt (like) / feel (like)
- note / noted / notice / noticed
- wonder / wondered
- experience / experienced
- seem / seemed / appear / appeared
- remember / remembered / recall / recalled

Here is a list of the "be verbs" and some "wanna be verbs" which often indicate a passive voice sentence (like this passive voice sentence – how ironic!):

Be Verbs	Wanna Be Verbs that show possession	Wanna Be Verbs – Telling, rather than showing POV character's mental status
Forms of to be – am, is, are, was, were, be, being, been similar verbs or parts of helping verbs – can, could, should, would, may, might, must, ought to, shall, will	contain (of), contain, include, involve, has / have, own, possess, etc.	agree, appear, believe, deny, disagree, doubt, forget, imagine, impress, know, mean, please, promise, realize, recognize, remember, suppose, think, understand

Eliminate miscellaneous filler words (often unnecessary):

	breathe / exhale / inhale	in spite of	quite	suddenly
bit	but	instead (of)	rather	slightly
a little	by the way / by way of	just	really	that
a lot	definitely	kind of	seriously	then
absolutely				
accordingly, according to	except	like (orally)	shrug	totally
actually	honestly	literally	since	try
almost	in addition to	now	slightly	well
basically	in front of	obviously	somehow	
because (of)	in place of	possibly	sort of	

BOOK MD EDITING

www.mirandadarrow.com

Step Six

What's Next?

The last step is working on your query package or preparing to self-publish. Most of this writing craft book applies the same regardless of your publishing plans and place in your writing career. But in Step Six, paths diverge. We'll have different sections for authors pursuing traditional publishing and for those planning to pursue indie publishing. Either way, this final step in the Six-Step Revision Process will help you prepare to send your manuscript into the world. If you're already under contract, send your manuscript to your acquiring editor early and make their day!

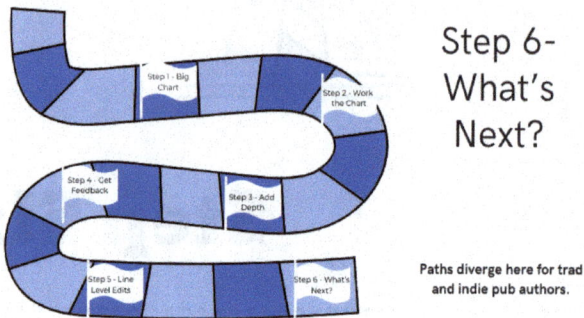

Step 6- What's Next?

Step 1 - Big Chart

Step 2 - Work the Chart

Step 4 - Get Feedback

Step 3 - Add Depth

Step 5 - Line Level Edits

Step 6 - What's Next?

Paths diverge here for trad and indie pub authors.

Make these steps work for *you*. You can start Step Six earlier, like when you are waiting to get feedback in Step Four. Get a jump on your book launch, query package, or whatever your next steps include once you have a solid grasp of your story and how you want to pitch it. Line up professionals (copyeditors, cover designers, etc.) in advance to get on their calendars.

Experienced authors, especially indie authors with their own planned release schedule, may start these Step Six tasks much earlier in the process. I know one indie author who had a preorder up before she'd even written the manuscript and had to keep her plot consistent with her blurb and cover that she'd already committed to. That stressed me out because it constrained the options for plot fixes. It presented a fun challenge, like an episode of *MacGyver*. You have a can opener, a roll of duct tape, and a pack of gum—make a novel.

Next steps for authors seeking traditional publication: If you're looking for traditional publishing, now is the time to work on your query package.

If you're contacting a literary agent or an acquiring editor at a traditional publishing company, here are the main query package materials:

- Query letter

- Synopsis (several lengths)

- Polished first pages

- A polished pitch for online writing/pitch events

- A list of agents to query, vet, and track when

they are open for queries

- Bulk chocolate and a comfy place to wait

The different materials required for querying agents is a big enough topic to be a separate book, so I am giving one paragraph on each and then moving on.

Query materials overview:

1. **Query Letter:** This should be a one-page letter pitching your story to an agent or acquiring editor. It should be single-spaced with empty lines between the paragraphs, 12-point font, and one-inch margins. Address it to the agent so they know you aren't sending this exact letter to everyone listed in the *Guide to Literary Agents* resource book. If you don't know someone's preferred pronouns, use their first and last name with no honorific (Mr., Ms., or Mx.). If the agent makes their honorifics clear on their website and submission requirements, follow that. One paragraph should be your book's metadata: the title (in ALL CAPS is most common), the word count (rounded to the nearest 1,000 words), the

age category and genre, and if possible two or three comp titles. Then two or three paragraphs maximum with your story blurb, capturing your main character, their goal, motivation, and conflict, the stakes if they fail, and the tough choice they will need to make. End with your brief author bio, two to three sentences including writing credits (shortlist only), and something about yourself showing you are a professional and would make a good client.

2. **Synopsis:** read the agent's submission requirements. Some do not want a synopsis at all. Some want one that is 500 words or less (approximately two pages double-spaced), or one single page. Follow these requirements. The synopsis is the outline of the major plot events in the story. Try to limit it to your main characters (five or less named in the synopsis) and the main plot (you can skip the subplots). Spoil the ending—don't be coy here. If you're pitching a romance, they want to know the emotional growth arc the lovers will go

through, along with the main external plot, plus that they will end up happy together. If you're pitching a mystery, agents want to know the main clues and actions plus what the sleuth does to solve the mystery (and that the mystery is solved at the end). If you're pitching fantasy or sci-fi, I know this is tough, but give only a brief (fifty words or less) description of the story's universe and how that impacts the main character's goal, the stakes, etc.

3. **First Pages:** read the agent's submission requirements. Some want ten or twenty pages, while others want five pages or 1,000 words. Some want fifty pages or the first three chapters. You need to send the right sample pages to show you are paying attention to the agent's rules. You are auditioning yourself as a client as well as your story as their next book to champion. Agents want authors who write many books, not just one, so the fit with the author is just as important as this story. The page count or word count listed is the *maximum*

you can send. End short if that is a better, grabbier, more compelling ending point. Do not end mid-sentence unless that's how the chapter ends. Leave the agent wanting to read more, desperate for you to send the full manuscript. I don't recommend copyediting for a full manuscript (unless you know that your grammar skills may be a barrier to agent interest) since traditional publishing companies will copyedit before publication. But I do recommend copyediting or seriously polishing these first pages (and your query letter and synopsis) so they're free from grammatical errors.

4. **Polish Your Pitch:** If you're attending a writing conference (in person or online) and can pitch your manuscript to agents, practice what you're going to say. Have a longer version if you get a pre-planned eight- to ten-minute pitch session (they go faster than you'd think) and practice a shorter thirty-second elevator pitch version in case you're seated at lunch with an agent who asks, "What are you working on?" Give

them the thirty-second version, not the five-minute one (unless they ask you for more details). If you're involved in an online pitch event, there are "rules" for those events too—character limits, hashtags, and preferred formats. Twitter/X has several events, as do other organizations like SavvyAuthors and the online pitch event for WFWA members. Get feedback from critique partners on your pitches before the event.

5. **List of Agents:** find agents that 1) work with your age category and genre, 2) are accepting submissions, 3) have a decent reputation, and 4) would be a good fit for your career and your personality. Just because someone likes your tweet during a pitch event does *not* mean that you have to send them anything or query them. Check them out first. You can find information about agents online: Google them, check the QueryTracker website, check the AuthorBeware website, check PublishersMarketplace (a paid service) to

see if they have any sales in your genre. One way to find agents is to see who represents the authors of your comp titles. They are usually thanked in a novel's acknowledgments. The *Guide to Literary Agents* resource book and the www.manuscriptwishlist.com website are other sources of information about agents.

Pepper, impatiently waiting, like me watching my inbox while querying.

Many freelance editors, including me, offer query package services. If you need help with your query materials, these services are available. I offer a package with all of these and have a special method of helping "snip your synopsis" to get it down to your target page or word count. I can also help you practice your pitch with a bit of roleplay, since I've been on the other side of that table (or screen) enough times to be able to ask the types of questions and know what you can do to be prepared for that pitch. To help you along the way, I've included a query status tracking spreadsheet in the Bonus Materials below. But no one can really prepare for all the waiting and rejections, so do engage in self-care while you are in the query trenches.

Next steps if you're self-publishing: now is the time to line up your group of professionals and fans to launch your book.

If you're indie publishing, line up your:

- Copyeditor/proofreader

- Cover designer

- Street team

- Ad and social media campaigns

- ARC giveaways

- Book cover-themed cake for your book launch

If this is your first time indie publishing, you will also need to set up:

- Kindle Direct Publishing account (or IngramSpark, or Lulu, and/or other distributors)

- Author Goodreads page

- Author page on Amazon

- Author website

Some indie authors have this process down with military precision. Others, less so. The good news is that you can learn as you go and work out your next steps so they fit perfectly for you.

Time to howl about your new release.

Here's a timeline one indie author shared, which I've tweaked a bit:

- Launch Date: Pick a date. For this example,

I'm using Dec 31st

- Draft and schedule posting of thank you messages on social media and emails for your launch team to send on launch day–1 day (Dec 30)

- Upload e-book cover and EPUB files on KDP (and other venues if "going wide")–15 days (Dec 16)

- Load print cover onto KDP (and/or other venues) along with updated file for print book–15 days (Dec 16)

- Research category and key terms for KDP and marketing–17 days (Dec 14)

- Finalize formatting of e-book and print book plus all versions of the cover–26 days (Dec 5)

- Upload audiobook on Audible and/or other venues–30 days (Dec 1)

- Upload print manuscript on KDP and order author proof copy–40 days (Nov 21)

- Send welcome email to launch team; start weekly reminder emails–41 days (Nov 20)

- Finalize audiobook recording–45 days (Nov 16)

- Prepare book launch team form; send invites to street team–46 days (Nov 15)

- Receive copyedits, work through and finalize manuscript–2 months (Oct 31)

- Send manuscript to copyeditor, have a concept discussion with cover artist–3 months (Sept 30)

- Finalize the book (including first five steps of this revision program)–3 months (Sept 30)

- Book time with your editor, cover designer, and/or promotion team as applicable–3-4 months in advance, if possible (Aug 30)

Freelance editors can help with your back cover copy, ad blurbs, and pull quotes for your social media promotions. Most editors have a waitlist, so plan ahead. Same for cover designers and formatters. Prep for your ad campaign and your street team early. As soon as you get your manuscript edited, send out your ARCs and get ready to launch.

Whew, we made it! The grandest of all chapter closing parties for completing the Six-Step Revision Process. We can use discarded drafts of our WIPs from the paper shredder as our ticker tape for this celebration.

The Bonus Content for Step Six is two spreadsheets:

1. For writers pursuing traditional publishing, there's a spreadsheet with columns to keep your query information in one place.

2. For indie publishing authors, there's an interactive indie book launch timeline calculator. It's a loaded spreadsheet. You enter your book launch date and it will calculate key dates for things to work on in advance, as it recalculates with any new

launch date you enter.

Bonus Content: Query Status Tracker Spreadsheet & Indie Launch Calculator

BOOK MD EDITING

Tracking list by [author name]
For [manuscript title]
Re: Query Tracking Chart
Date of first query sent: September 22, 2024
Date of most recent update to chart [add date]

Agent name	Literary agency	link for querying - email or	Date of query	Nudge date/date	Pass = pass for agency	Response to query letter (R/P/NRDN)

BOOK MD EDITING

To: AUTHOR
From: Miranda Darrow, Book MD Editing
Re: Countdown to Launch Calculator
Date: September 19, 2024

Categories	Dates	Status updates	adjusted dates if nec: indicate when completed
Launch Date - insert your date into cell b:12	31-Dec-24		
Draft and schedule posting of thank you messages on SM and emails for launch team to send la	30-Dec-24		
Upload e-book Cover and EPUB on KDP (and other venues if wide)	16-Dec-24		
Load print cover onto KDP along with update file for print book (other venues)	16-Dec-24		
Research Category & Key Terms for KDP and marketing	14-Dec-24		
Finalize formatting of e-book and print book plus all versions of the cover	5-Dec-24		
Audiobook upload on audible, other venues	1-Dec-24		
Upload print manuscript on KDP & order author proof copy	21-Nov-24		
Welcome email to launch team, start of weekly reminder emails	20-Nov-24		
Audiobook recording finalized	16-Nov-24		
Book launch team form ready, send invites to street crew	15-Nov-24		
Receive copyedits, work through and finalize manuscript	31-Oct-24		
Send manuscript to copyeditor/concept discussion with cover artist	30-Sep-24		
Finalize your book (including first five steps of this revision program)	30-Sep-24		
Book time with your editor, cover designer, audiobook voice actor, and/or promotion team	31-Aug-24		

Motivation & Checklist

Bonus Materials link

Whew, we made it through the Six Steps. Piece of cake, right? Not really. It's been a lot of work. Sometimes we try things and realize that we're not a natural prodigy at everything we want to do. My husband signed us up for a couples' bowling league. I've never bowled more than once a year, and I was never particularly good. But I got a bowling ball and shoes. The shoes were worth it—not having to rent shoes every week, plus fashion!

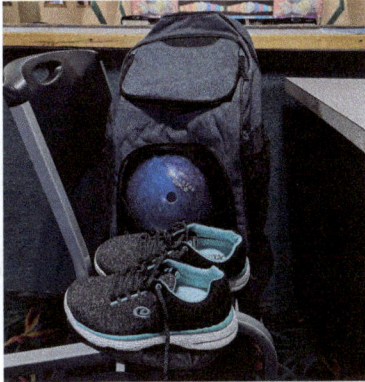

Miranda's bowling ball, shoes, and the alley of many humiliations.

We tried going on non-league days so I could practice, but I was still awful (the whole season, I only broke 100 twice). But I got a little bit better and learned to not be so embarrassed. I was proving that my 135-point handicap was earned and that I wasn't faking a lack of bowling skills to hustle the league. At the end of the season, I got an award for having the second-best score compared to handicap for one of my games. I'm still undeniably awful. It was an improvement and I survived.

Here's where I encourage you to dig deep and remember that you *can* do the hard things. Right now, make a list of four things you've done in your life, whether it's an accomplishment you've earned or just a tough situation that you survived. My list, like most people's (especially anyone with decades of opportunities for stuff to happen in life) is much longer than four.

Here are some I include when I need a reminder that I can do the hard things:

- I've worked for law firms and corporations, showing up every day despite being a cog in a machine.

- I lost my mother a few years back at the height of COVID.

- My family drove twenty-six straight hours to make it to my brother's wedding in Florida when our flight from Minnesota was canceled.

- I finished reading *Wanderers* (apologies to Chuck Wendig, but it's 854 pages—that was a feat).

Now it's your turn. Think about some hard things you've been through or past accomplishments. You don't need to list four—go with what works for you.

Dig deep and think about things that took time and effort.

1.

2.

3.

4.

You've made it through these tough things. Revising your manuscript is easier, less painful, and totally worth it.

Whatever shows up on your list, even if it's minor things like *I made my bed today* or *I aim to be polite to my in-laws*, that stuff is hard and (here's the kicker) it doesn't result in you having a manuscript that you

Name and claim your past wins!

can be proud of. The hard stuff you've already done likely has perks, but none of them are getting you a polished, ready-to-query or ready to indie publish novel. Revising your manuscript is work. The results are worth it if you put in the effort.

You are not attempting to boil the ocean with a candle. You have the knowledge and skills to do

this. And now, you also have a framework and a checklist (see below). Check those boxes. Move on down the Six Steps. Keep moving forward.

And the good news: it gets easier as you learn and improve through repetition. You'll likely:

- Be more mindful of story structure while drafting.

- Learn the fundamentals for correct punctuation of dialogue so you won't need to fix it in later manuscripts.

- Become more mindful of POV and verb tense choice, reducing the angst of shifting POV and verb tense in a whole manuscript.

- Think about setting when you're writing scenes and at least make some notes for your future self [add boardroom or enchanted forest or dystopian hellscape description here].

Good luck with your writing!

This checklist and all of the Bonus Content are available as free downloads available through this QR code and accessible via the link to the bonus page on my website:

https://www.mirandadarrow.com/books/six-step -page

> **Bonus Content: Six-Step Revision Process Checklist**

BOOK MD EDITING

Miranda Darrow's Six-Step Revision Process Checklist

- ☐ Step 1 - Make the "Big Chart" in format of your choice:
  - ☐ Capture all the current scenes main plot, character growth, etc.
  - ☐ Identify missing key scenes, add chart rows
  - ☐ Tag for "rehoming" those darlings that aren't moving story forward
  - ☐ Map out your developmental/story level revision plan
- ☐ Step 2 - Work the Chart – revise for developmental editing topics:
  - ☐ Plot – Cohesive story with logical progression
    - ○ Wrap up loose ends
    - ○ Subplots tie into main story
  - ☐ Pacing – consult beat sheet or resource if needed
  - ☐ Character growth arc for each POV character:
    - ○ Clarify POV character(s) GMC and how it evolves
    - ○ Necessary backstory as foundation for emotional wound
    - ○ Challenge and overcome this emotional wound (if positive – or don't if negative)
- ☐ Step 3 - Add Depth - Paragraph-level edits:
  - ☐ Setting – get the "right amount" to add texture without bogging down pacing
  - ☐ Dialogue –goal = able to identify all main character's lines just by their lines, word choice
  - ☐ Show, Don't Tell
    - ○ Key Scenes during story timeline appear "live" on page, not told later
    - ○ Character emotion & feelings – demonstrate, rather than name
- ☐ Step 4 - Get feedback:
  - ☐ Critique Partners and/or Beta Readers
  - ☐ Incorporate Feedback - Evaluate what recommendations to implement, second opinion if needed
- ☐ Step 5 - Line edits:
  - ☐ Active Voice/Active Verbs
  - ☐ Copyedit (spelling, grammar, usage, punctuation, consistency)
- ☐ Step 6 - What's Next:
  - ☐ Seeking Trad pub OR Indie authors
  - ☐ Send your polished manuscript into the world!

About the Concise Fiction Academy Series

- -

As a freelance editor, I've worked with countless authors, methodically teasing out the best versions of their manuscripts. As a practicing corporate attorney for the past twenty-eight years, including fifteen years in-house at a corporation, one of my main responsibilities is explaining complex issues clearly and concisely, translating the issues from legal jargon to plain language with process maps, charts, and other tools that speak to businesspeople. Too many details can dilute or divert the stakeholders from the "important bits." My communications need to help my audience keep their focus on the big picture while pointing out where they can go for more details on various sub-topics.

There are tons of writing craft books, including a handful on revising your novel. Many of these craft books are good and very thorough. So thorough that I, a super-reader who reads at least 150 published books a year (not to mention the unpublished books I work on each year), have a hard time finishing some. Too many pages, steps, and words (and not enough templates, pictures, charts, and checklists). There are already great craft books, but what I feel is missing is something more concise and accessible to busy authors seeking writing craft books shorter than their WIPs. That's what I can add to this discussion. Each book in the Concise Fiction Academy series will focus on a different aspect of writing craft and offer a clear and concise high-level explanation of complex fiction writing topics.

I'm currently collecting opening pages to feature in an upcoming book in the series: *Unputdownable Openings*. For my examples, I'm accessing public domain stories and first pages with permission. This could be

Nominate your first page.

your book, with your opening page featured in a positive light in my upcoming craft book. Note: all selected openings will be highlighted as positive examples of a specific aspect of creating a compelling opening and will include your name, title, and author website. If you're a published author (trad or indie) and would like your first page considered for inclusion, please fill out the form linked on my website at: https://www.mirandadarrow.com/books/ This form will remain open until my book on opening pages is completed, to the extent any book is ever "final."

I'm working on a few more titles right now. Let me know which future books in the series you want to see soon:

- Gameify Your Writing to Level Up Your Productivity

- Dash of Love—Adding a Romantic Subplot to Your Novel of Any Genre

- Unputdownable Openings

- Writing Catchy Dialogue

- "Show, Don't Tell" Made Simple

- Pick the Perfect Point of View (POV) for Your Novel

- Worldbuilding and Immersive Setting for all Fiction Genres

- Various Plotting Methods Summarized and Compared

- Construct Your Universe Bible: a Worldbuilding Bootcamp for Sci-Fi and Fantasy

- Using Tropes in Romance

- Edge of Their Seats: Writing Mystery, Suspense, and Thrillers

- Developmental Editing Concepts and Deliverables

- Something else? I'm open to suggestions.

It may seem counterintuitive for a freelance fiction editor to write a book showing authors a process for efficiently and relatively painlessly revising their manuscripts, decreasing or eliminating the need for professional editors. Hiring experienced and talented editors is the gold standard, but not all authors can afford to have an editor give individualized attention to their work. As an editor dedicated to the writing community, I want to make quality writing craft and editing resources available to writers across the resource spectrum, which is why I'm writing this line of shorter writing craft books with a modest price for e-books.

Giving back to the writing community is also why I volunteer with the RevPit online writing contest every year. The RevPit family of editors runs a free online writing event with lots of writing tips and advice, with the contest winners receiving free developmental edits of their full manuscripts. For more information on RevPit visit our website at www.reviseresub.com, subscribe to our Substack email list, and follow our subreddit group.

Gratitudes

First, I want to thank you, the writer reading this book. Indie publishing writing craft books is a new adventure for me, and I want to thank you for joining me on this wild ride. I hope to someday build this into a valuable series for writers who want to learn about writing craft in more digestible chunks, whether they find me online on social media or see me presenting at a writing conference. If you like what you read, please post a review.

Goodreads https://bit.ly/Goodreads6SRP

Amazon https://amzn.to/3SjsFRR

Feel free to post a review even if you don't find it useful: reviews are for readers, not authors. This is a bit of a conundrum when my audience is authors, but there you go. This book wouldn't have been possible without the support of my writing family. I want to thank my critique partners and friends Kristen Ray, Despina Karras, and Madelyn Knecht, who read and critiqued this book. I also want to thank my friend and critique partner Diane Wiggs who consulted on many iterations of my cover art, which was created by 100Covers.com. Many thanks to Alice Douthwaite of www.Paper-FreeEditing.com for her careful proofreading on a tight deadline. Even editors need editors, and Alice came through for me in a pinch!

Pepper, ready for adoration.

I want to thank my RevPit family of editors who've taught me so much about editing and running a freelance editing business, especially my fellow board members Jeni Chappelle, Carly Hayward, Natasha Hanova, Maria Tureaud, and Joel Brigham. A special shout-out to my unofficial editing mentor, Jennifer Lawler from ClubEdFreelancers.com. Jennifer's Classes and Products for Freelance Editors gave me the tools and feedback so I had the confidence to publish this book. I also want to thank Alexa Bigwarfe for including me in her Women in Publishing Summit and author community which has been immensely helpful.

The book wouldn't have been possible without the support of my non-writing family, my husband, our teen sons, and Pepper, the dog who rules us all.

About the Author

Miranda Darrow is an award-winning author who lives in central Minnesota with her husband, teen sons, and a bossy little dog who rules the roost. She enjoys camping, boating,

Miranda Darrow

playing piano, and foisting
her crochet projects onto everyone she encounters.

Miranda is a freelance fiction editor and #RevPit online revision contest board member and contributing editor. She's also a frequent presenter to writing groups and may be available to present to your writing group online or in person. For more information, see her editing website: www.mirandadarrow.com